The New   MO

About the Book

Now published in the enlar
and reliable source of inform
road-going motorcycles. Its
technical specifications provi   both for
those who know about bikes   who want to learn
about them. Manufacturers are   alphabetically by name
and a representative cross-section of their model line-up is
arranged in engine size order. In trying to picture an industry
which is dominated by a few major producers who export
across the world but also includes many small-scale, national
manufacturers, inevitably some selection from the total available model range has been made.

The fifth edition of this practical reference book lists most
of the 1985-6 road bikes and provides a reliable consumer
guide to the world motorcycle industry. The book includes
some mopeds and scooters because definitions of motorcycles vary from country to country and, in any case, two
wheel road-users have much in common and share a unique
experience. Some of the machines featured are dual purpose
machines capable of being ridden on road and across country.
Most manufacturers also include in their range machines
which are strictly for off-road racing and these are not in-
cluded in this book.

About the Author

Robert Croucher writes about motorcycles because he enjoys
riding them, he is fascinated by the history of their development, he admires the daring of those who race them and he
is intrigued by the ingenuity of design that goes into their
manufacture. His own riding experience on Hondas, Ducatis
and, more recently, BMWs has convinced him that the road-
craft skills and understanding that come with regular biking
are a very appropriate preparation for the motorist.

He believes the book will have served a purpose if it settles
an argument over technical matters, demonstrates some of the
variety of character of motorcycles in the 1980s, or inspires
the reader to look more closely at what motorcycling can offer
as an experience in an energy and safety-conscious world.

As well as the paperback *New Observer's* guides, there are hardback *Observers* too, covering a wide range of topics.

NATURAL HISTORY   Birds   Birds' Eggs   Wild Animals
Farm Animals   Sea Fishes   Butterflies   Larger Moths
Caterpillars   Sea and Seashore   Cats   Trees   Grasses
Cacti   Gardens   Roses   House Plants   Vegetables
Geology   Fossils

SPORT AND LEISURE   Golf   Tennis   Sea Fishing
Music   Folk Song   Jazz   Big Bands   Sewing   Furniture
Architecture   Churches

COLLECTING   Awards and Medals   Glass   Pottery and
Porcelain   Silver   Victoriana   Firearms   Kitchen Antiques

TRANSPORT   Small Craft   Canals   Vintage Cars   Classic
Cars   Manned Spaceflight   Unmanned Spaceflight

TRAVEL AND HISTORY   London   Devon and Cornwall
Cotswolds   World Atlas   European Costume   Ancient
Britain   Heraldry

The New Observer's Book of

Motorcycles

Robert M. Croucher

Frederick Warne

FREDERICK WARNE
Penguin Books Ltd, Harmondsworth, Middlesex, England
Viking Penguin Inc., 40 West 23rd Street, New York, New York 10010, U.S.A.
Penguin Books Australia Ltd, Ringwood, Victoria, Australia
Penguin Books Canada Ltd, 2801 John Street, Markham, Ontario, Canada L3R 1B4
Penguin Books (N.Z.) Ltd, 182–190 Wairau Road, Auckland 10, New Zealand

First published 1976
Fifth edition 1986

Originally published as *The Observer's Book of Motorcycles*
in small hardback format

ISBN 0 7232 1697 5

Printed and bound in Great Britain by
Butler & Tanner Ltd
Frome and London

Introduction to the Fifth Edition

The fifth edition of this book brings together another rich collection of the world's motorcycles for the biking enthusiast to observe. The machines featured vary from 50 cc mopeds to full-dress tourers, with engines developing between 1.4 and 130 brake horsepower and costing from under £300 to over £9 000.

Motorcycle design has always been proved on the track but the styling theme for the 1980s clearly shows its racing origins with the Grand Prix replicas that feature in most model ranges. The adrenalin fix that comes to bikers through the right hand has been boosted by many of the current models. Their power-to-weight ratio advantage and efficient aerodynamics mean that many of them can out-accelerate the most powerful of sports cars. At least fifty of the standard road-going machines featured in this book can reach over 200 km/h ridden hard. Remarkably, this super performance comes now from more compact engines. Manufacturers have turned away from mighty cubic capacity to seek performance through greater engine efficiency and lightweight frame design. Ten years ago the Honda CB750F produced 67 bhp from its 736 cc four-cylinder engine and was labelled a "superbike". The 1985 Honda CBX750F is lighter by 23 kg and can squeeze 90 bhp from its slimline, 748 cc vee-four power plant. The 82 horsepower of the Kawasaki Z900, a king of the roadburners in the mid-seventies, now looks almost under-powered against the 115 bhp output of the present GPz 900R.

How far manufacturers should go in pushing up the power output of road-going machines is one of the current issues of the biking world. Some countries have suggested a 100 bhp limit following the informal arrangement West Germany made with importers to restrict horsepower, and it seems that the manufacturers themselves may decide to draw the line at 125 bhp. Not that this need worry performance seekers because Yamaha's FZ750, a 4-stroke that thinks it is a racing 2-stroke, can top 230 km/h with its 100 bhp engine.

In contrast to the early seventies when increases in engine power looked likely to outstrip the frame technology, 1985–6 models are designed to handle performance in a total way. The awesome engine power is contained within strong, race-developed frames, controlled by powerful disc brake systems and fully-adjustable suspensions, and put on to the tarmac through tyre designs that afford grip in both the wet and the dry. The outstanding question is not how genuine are these GP replica roadsters, but whether their "boy racer" owners have the riding skills to handle them properly on busy roads. The biking image has always been strong on personal freedoms and such responsive performance in road machines begs to be ridden hard and fast.

Dressed as for the track in colourful leathers and matching helmet and astride a Honda NS400R or Suzuki RG500 Gamma, it takes but a slight flight of fancy for the rider to see each set of traffic lights on the road as the starting grid at Assen or Monza.

The history of motorcycling has been one of peaks and troughs in popularity. The fifth edition of the *Observer's Book of Motorcycles* emerges at a time when bike sales are struggling to retain the levels established in the 1970s. The optimism of the major world suppliers that the motorcycle market was expandable has suffered some re-assessment since 1980. 1983 was a particular set back for the Japanese giants of the trade. Yamaha saw its bike sales slump by 60 per cent and firms such as Honda and Suzuki stayed in profit only because of the help from their car business. Such tough times caused several smaller manufacturers around the world to run into serious financial difficulties. 1984 produced bike production crises for a number of famous marques, such as Bultaco, Ducati, Fantic, Laverda, Maico, Montesa, Ossa and Zündapp. This fall in sales resulted partly from the general economic recession hitting the consumer market, but some of the losses stemmed from the marketing war that many manufacturers allowed to break out in an attempt to clear the over-capacity by fiercely competitive discounting.

The main technical developments since the 1982 edition of this book have concentrated on giving bikes extra performance in an easily handled package. The earlier trend towards turbo-charging has yielded to the adoption of slim, highly efficient motors married to frames and steering geometry developed for the track to give total performance. The variety of engine configurations has never been greater, and considerable design ingenuity has been used in research and development to increase power output and yet deliver it in a smooth, manageable way. The result is that many of the new bike engines are responsive across a broad band of high-to-low speed pulling power without the need for frequent gear-changing. Clever exhaust valve technology has been linked with faster-breathing carburation to obtain high compression ratios with maximum combustion efficiency. Several models from the BMW and Kawasaki ranges feature car-type, digital fuel injection, controlled by on-board micro-processors, to provide an optimum fuel mixture to the engine under all operating conditions. Motorcycle electronics are more widely used for ignition control where they are able to offer greater performance and more reliability than conventional mechanical methods.

Tougher anti-noise regulations for motorcycles in Europe and North America have proved to be difficult to meet for existing air-cooled engines, and liquid-cooling has become more popular as a means towards muffling power plant noise. To house these powerful engines, high-tensile, box section steels have been used to improved chassis strength without unduly increasing weight. The need to eliminate frame flexing on the race track led to the creation of space frames for road bikes that remain rigid under all handling stresses. They contribute to aerodynamic efficiency because of the reduced frontal area of the design. Handling has been improved also by anti-dive systems which prevent the front fork from over-reacting to sudden braking. At the rear, the progressive action, single shock suspension systems that were first introduced on motocross racers have become a widely-adopted standard. Powerful motorcycles need responsive brakes and the state of the art remains the triple-disc and dual-piston caliper system with sintered metal pads for all-weather capability. Anti-lock braking is still at the development stage for motorcycles, although systems have been used, with positive results, on police machines.

Tyre developments have introduced the first radial or belted tyres for high-performance bikes. At extreme speeds the conventional cross-ply design deforms and the heat build-up leads to increased wear and reduced road grip. Pirelli, first into the market with radials for road bikes, claim that the belted design stabilises tread pattern distortion and can extend tyre life by up to 50 per cent. Bike bodywork, once an after-sales accessory provided by specialist firms, comes now factory-fitted with colour-matched fairing and belly pans. This dressing not only combines aerodynamics with some weather protection for the rider, but it also captures the all-important styling image of the race track. The most comprehensive vision of bodywork on bikes is provided by the big tourers with their stereo-radio equipped fairings and colour-matched top boxes and pannier luggage. They may also be seen towing a luggage trailer, now legal in the United Kingdom at speeds of up to 80 km/h.

As with its previous editions, this book has been made possible by the helpful co-operation of the manufacturers and my thanks are extended for this assistance. While every effort has been made to ensure the book's accuracy it is not possible to guarantee all specifications because the manufacturers reserve the right to alter model details without notice. The motorcycles featured in this fifth edition are in most cases from the 1985 ranges and are built to UK or European market specifications.

Robert M. Croucher

Technical Specifications Explained

How to use this book

Model: Manufacturers identify each model in their bike range by a code made up of letters and numbers. Sometimes a model also gets a name. The code describes the type of bike, its engine capacity and may indicate a special feature or the year of its introduction. Model codes are not standardised and names such as Super, GP or Custom may mean different things to each manufacturer.

Engine: Motorcycle engines come in single- or multi-cylinder form and as 2- or 4-strokes. 2-strokes are also classified by their intake system as piston port, reed or rotary disc valve, while 4-strokes are described by their valve actuating mechanism as overhead valve (ohv), single (sohc) or double (dohc) overhead camshafts. Single cylinder engines normally sit vertically in the frame sloping slightly forward but multi-cylinder engine blocks can be arranged in-line across the frame, in a vee or flat formation to create twins, triples, fours and, sometimes, sixes. LC indicates liquid cooling normally by water jacket and radiator.
Capacity: The cubic content of the cylinder(s) in centimetres. This measure of engine size may be significant for taxation, insurance and safety legislation purposes. Learner riders in the UK are restricted to bikes of under 125 cc capacity.
Bore × Stroke: A measure of the relationship between the cylinder head diameter and the length of the piston within it in millimetres. Modern motorcycle engines are often short stroke and square. Long stroke thumping is characteristic of big touring bikes.
Compression ratio: A measure of the compression of the fuel/air mixture in each cylinder by the rising piston before ignition. A high compression engine would have a ratio of 9:1 or over.
Carburettor: This meters fuel and air to the engine. The number of carburettors, the choke size diameter and the make are given. The carburettor may be of the slide or constant velocity (CV) type.
Maximum power: The brake horsepower (bhp) and the engine speed (rpm) at which it is achieved. This figure can vary with the methods used to measure it. Most of the figures used in this book are German DIN standard which measures the net output of the engine at the flywheel under normal use conditions with pumps and generators working. In the UK 12 bhp is used as a legal limit for learner bikes.
Starting: Invariably by push button electric starters. Some bikes retain the kick-operated crank and mopeds may be started using their pedals.

Transmission: The number of gears in the gearbox and the method of final drive to the rear wheel. Most bikes use a wet, multi-plate clutch to engage and disengage engine drive. Mopeds and scooters often use centrifugal clutches to give a completely automatic drive.

Electrics: The bike voltage system which is normally now 12 v. The ignition system which is commonly transistorised and maintenance-free and the battery capacity in ampere-hours (Ah). Batteries are usually charged by an alternator. Some lightweight machines still use a 6 v system with a flywheel magneto for generating ignition current and a small dry cell battery for lighting.

Frame: Commonly, a strong tubular steel frame formed in a single or double cradle. A duplex frame has two front down tubes. Many high performance bikes now feature square or box section frames combining strength with rigidity. Some mopeds use pressed steel spines with the engine acting as a stressed member. Scooters often have an integral, monocoque body construction.

Suspension: Front suspension is usually by telescopic fork with compression and rebound damping by coil springs and hydraulic pressure. Some big bikes supplement this system with infinitely variable air pressure. Anti-dive systems further control the compression damping of the front fork under severe braking. Conventionally, rear suspension is by swinging arm and hydraulic shock absorbers. The single shock system, designed originally for motocross racers, is used now on a number of road machines. Trade names include Honda's *Pro-Link*, Kawasaki's *Uni-Trak*, Suzuki's *Full-Floater* and Yamaha's *Monocross*. Uniquely, BMW's *Monoshock* system comprises a torsionally rigid single swinging arm with one offset shock absorber. Both spring pre-load and damping characteristics of the rear shock absorbers may be adjustable.

Brakes: Braking can be drum or disc operated. The hydraulic disc brake is now the more commonly used system. Recent advances in disc brake technology include the use of drilled discs, the dual-piston brake caliper (d-pc), float mounted discs, ventilated rear discs and Moto Guzzi's integral braking system which links front and rear discs through the foot pedal to provide balanced and efficient braking.

Tyres: Traditionally, motorcycle wheels are wire spoked but the industry standard is changing to cast aluminium alloy in a variety of styles. Tubeless tyres have been possible on motorcycles since the introduction of cast wheels. Front tyres are often smaller and narrower than the rear tyres. Front tyres are ribbed to give positive steering ability while the rear rubber is broader with a curved profile and deep zig-zag treads to transmit the power during acceleration and to grip the road on cornering. Tyre sizes are indicated in a variety of ways. A size of 3.50–18 indicates the tyre width and the wheelrim diameter in inches. A tyre may also be designated as 100/90V–18 where the 100 measures the tyre width in millimetres, the 90 is a percentage and refers to the ratio between the height of the tyre and its width, and the 18 is the wheelrim diameter in inches. Other tyre markings include V which shows that the tyre is suitable for high speeds exceeding 200 km/h, H for high performance up to 200 km/h and S for standard road tyres. These speed ratings are based on correct inflation on the right rim size wheel and being run within their designed load capacity.

Dimensions: Metric measures are provided as illustrated in the following diagram:

The *Fuel tank* figure is a maximum and usually includes 2–3 litres in reserve.

The *Dry weight* figure provides a standard so that bikes can be compared regardless of any differences in fuel or oil capacity.

Performance: Most manufacturers are reluctant to give performance figures for their motorcycles because what can be achieved clearly varies with the rider, and is dependent on the conditions under which the testing is carried out. The examples quoted are based, in many cases, on published test results and should be read as approximate limits rather than absolute standards. Fuel consumption figures, in particular, can be very misleading when they are obtained under conditions of steady, slow-speed running. The figures given are based on an expected litres consumption over a distance of 100 kilometres and are only a rough guide to what might be obtained under typical, mixed riding conditions.

Features: Similar models with alternative styling or engine capacity, and details of any special equipment fitted as standard.

... indicates that information is not available.

AJS (UK)

Model: Enduro/Trail 250

Engine: 2-str Rotax single
Capacity: 248 cc
Bore × Stroke: 72 × 61 mm
Compression ratio: 13.5:1
Carburettor: 34 mm Mikuni
Maximum power: 37.5 bhp
(DIN) at 7 750 rpm
Starting: kick

Transmission: 5-speed with
chain drive

Electrics: Bosch CDI 12 v
ignition

Frame: Duplex tubular cradle

Suspension: Telehydraulic
front fork with rear *Girling* gas
shocks

Brakes: Drums front and rear

Tyres: Front is 2.75–21
Rear is 4.00–18

Dimensions:
Length: 2 108 mm
Width: 838 mm
Wheelbase: 1 422 mm
Clearance: 304 mm
Seat height: 914 mm
Dry weight: 99.8 kg
Fuel tank: 11.3 litres

Performance:
Top speed: ...
Fuel consumption: ...

Features: ...

Manufacturer: F. B. AJS of Andover Ltd, Goodworth Clatford,
Andover, Hants SP11 7RP, England.

AMAZONAS (Brazil)

Model: AME 1600

Engine: 4-str LC 8-valve VW
flat twin
Capacity: 1 581 cc
Bore × Stroke: 85.5 × 69 mm
Compression ratio: 7.2:1
Carburettor: 2/32 mm Solex
Maximum power: 50 bhp
(DIN) at 4 000 rpm
Starting: electric

Transmission: 4-speed with
chain drive and reverse gear

Electrics: Coil ignition 12 v
with 36 Ah battery

Frame: Duplex tubular cradle

Suspension: Telehydraulic
front fork with rear *VW shocks*
and helical springs

Brakes: Triple disc system

Tyres: Front is 4.50–16
Rear is 5.00–16

Dimensions:
Length: 2 480 mm
Width: 800 mm
Wheelbase: 1 680 mm
Clearance: 130 mm
Seat height: ...
Dry weight: 386 kg
Fuel tank: 20 litres

Performance:
Top speed: 175 km/h
Fuel consumption: 10 l/100 km

Features: Unique side car
outfit built by Koch Motorrad-
Schlagdstrasse 31–33, D-3442
Wanfried, West Germany.

Manufacturer: Amazonas, rua Bernardo Ramos 60, 6900 Manaus,
Brazil, South America.

APRILIA (Italy)

Model: ETX 600

Engine: 4-str LC 4-valve
single
Capacity: 561.83 cc
Bore × Stroke: 94 × 81 mm
Compression ratio: 9.6:1
Carburettor: 40 mm Dell'Orto
Maximum power: 49 bhp
(DIN) at 7 250 rpm
Starting: electric

Transmission: 5-speed with
chain drive

Electrics: Transistorised 12 v
ignition

Frame: Split single beam

Suspension: Telehydraulic
front fork with rear gas
monoshock *Aprilia Progressive
System*

Brakes: 260 mm front disc
with d-pc and rear disc

Tyres: Front is 3.00–21MT49
Rear is 5.10–17MT49

Dimensions:
Length: 2 200 mm
Width: 860 mm
Wheelbase: 1 480
Clearance: 300 mm
Seat height: 890 mm
Dry weight: 139 kg
Fuel tank: 14 litres

Performance:
Top speed: 160 km/h
Fuel consumption: 4.3 l/100 km

Features: Also as 350 cc
model. Acoustic alarm for side
stand.

Manufacturer: Aprilia S.p.A., via G. Galilei 1, 30033 Noale (VE),
Italy.

APRILIA (Italy)

Model: AS 125R

Engine: 2-str LC Rotax RAVE single
Capacity: 123.6 cc
Bore × Stroke: 54 × 54 mm
Compression ratio: 14.2:1
Carburettor: 28 mm Dell'Orto
Maximum power: 26 bhp (DIN) at 8 500 rpm
Starting: kick

Transmission: 6-speed with chain drive

Electrics: Transistorised 12 v ignition

Frame: Duplex tubular cradle

Suspension: Telescopic front fork with *APS* rear monoshock system

Manufacturer: Aprilia S.p.A.

Brakes: 240 mm front disc and 230 mm rear disc

Tyres: Front is 100/90-16 A55
Rear is 100/90-18 M55

Dimensions:
Length: 2 015 mm
Width: 750 mm
Wheelbase: 1 365 mm
Clearance: ...
Seat Height: 800 mm
Dry weight: 107 kg
Fuel tank: 11.5 litres

Performance:
Top speed: 127 km/h
Fuel consumption: 4 l/100 km

Features: RAVE—Rotax Automatic Variable Exhaust valve control.

APRILIA (Italy)

Model: EXT 125

Engine: 2-str LC Rotax single
Capacity: 123.6 cc
Bore × Stroke: 54 × 54 mm
Compression ratio: 14.2:1
Carburettor: 20 mm Dell'Orto
Maximum power: 22 bhp
(DIN) at 8 000 rpm
Starting: kick

Transmission: 6-speed with chain drive

Electrics: Transistorised 12 v ignition

Frame: Split single beam

Suspension: Telescopic front fork with *APS* rear monoshock system

Manufacturer: Aprilia S.p.A.

Brakes: 230 mm front disc and 125 mm rear drum

Tyres: Front is 2.75–21
Rear is 4.00–18

Dimensions:
Length: 2 130 mm
Width: 860 mm
Wheelbase: 1 450 mm
Clearance: ...
Seat height: 875 mm
Dry weight: 113 kg
Fuel tank: 10 litres

Performance:
Top speed: 125 km/h
Fuel consumption: 4 l/100 km

Features: ...

APRILIA (Italy)

Model: Tuareg 50

Engine: 2-str LC Rotax single
Capacity: 49.6 cc
Bore × Stroke: 38.8 × 42 mm
Compression ratio: 11:1
Carburettor: 12 mm Dell'Orto
Maximum power: 1.5 bhp
(DIN) at 3 750 rpm
Starting: kick

Transmission: 4-speed with
chain drive

Electrics: Transistorised 12 v
ignition

Frame: Split single beam

Suspension: Telescopic front
fork with *APS* rear monoshock
system

Manufacturer: Aprilia S.p.A.

Brakes: 230 mm front disc
and 118 mm rear drum

Tyres: Front is 2.75–21
Rear is 3.50–18

Dimensions:
Length: 2 070 mm
Width: 805 mm
Wheelbase: 1 330 mm
Clearance: ...
Seat height: 845 mm
Dry weight: 80 kg
Fuel tank: 18 litres

Performance:
Top speed: 40 km/h
Fuel consumption: 2 l/100 km

Features: Also as 125 cc and
250 cc models.

BATAVUS (The Netherlands)

Model: Mondial

Engine: 2-str reed valve single
Capacity: 49 cc
Bore × Stroke: 38 × 42 mm
Compression ratio: 9:1
Carburettor: 12 mm Gurtner
Maximum power: 2.4 bhp
(DIN) at 5 000 rpm
Starting: pedal

Transmission: Variable speed
automatic with chain drive

Electrics: Flywheel magneto
6 v ignition

Frame: Pressed steel spine

Suspension: Telescopic front
fork with twin rear dampers

Brakes: 90 mm drums
front and rear

Tyres: 2.25–16,
front and rear

Dimensions:
Length: ...
Width: 845 mm
Wheelbase: 1 320 mm
Clearance: ...
Seat height: ...
Dry weight: 44 kg
Fuel tank: 3.5 litres

Performance:
Top speed: 48 km/h
Fuel consumption: 1.7 l/100 km

Features: ...

Manufacturer: Batavus Intercycle B.V., Po 515, NL-8440
Heerenveen, The Netherlands.

BENELLI (Italy)

Model: 900 Sei

Engine: 4-str sohc in-line six
Capacity: 905.9 cc
Bore × Stroke: 60 × 53.4 mm
Compression ratio: 9.5:1
Carburettor: 3/24 mm Dell'Orto
Maximum power: 80 bhp
(DIN) at 8 400 rpm
Starting: electric

Transmission: 5-speed with
chain drive

Electrics: Transistorised 12 v
ignition with 28 Ah battery

Frame: Duplex tubular cradle

Suspension: Telescopic front
fork and rear adjustable
hydraulic shocks

Brakes: 300 mm dual front
discs and 260 mm rear disc

Tyres: Front is 100/90V–18
Rear is 120/90V–18

Dimensions:
Length: 2 110 mm
Width: 690 mm
Wheelbase: 1 460 mm
Clearance: 150 mm
Seat height: 790 mm
Dry weight: 220 kg
Fuel tank: 16.5 litres

Performance:
Top speed: 215 km/h
Fuel consumption: 8 l/100 km

Features: Linked braking
system.

Manufacturer: F.lli Benelli S.p.A., Chiusa di Ginestreto, 61100
Pesaro, Italy.

BENELLI (Italy)

Model: 654

Engine: 4-str sohc in-line four
Capacity: 604 cc
Bore × Stroke: 60 × 53.4 mm
Compression ratio: 9.3:1
Carburettor: 4/22 mm Dell'Orto
Maximum power: 62 bhp
(DIN) at 8 650 rpm
Starting: electric

Transmission: 5-speed with
chain drive

Electrics: 12 v coil ignition
with 12 Ah battery

Frame: Duplex tubular cradle

Suspension: Telescopic front
fork and rear 3-way adjustable
hydraulic shocks

Manufacturer: F.lli Benelli S.p.A.

Brakes: 260 mm triple disc
system with linked braking

Tyres: Front is 3.255S–18
Rear is 3.50S–18

Dimensions:
Length: 2 090 mm
Width: 787 mm
Wheelbase: 1 410 mm
Clearance: 150 mm
Seat height: 790 mm
Dry weight: 182 kg
Fuel tank: 15 litres

Performance:
Top speed: 190 km/h
Fuel consumption: 6 l/100 km

Features: Also as sports
version.

BENELLI (Italy)

Model: 304

Engine: 4-str sohc in-line four
Capacity: 231.1cc
Bore × Stroke: 45.5 × 38 mm
Compression ratio: 10.6:1
Carburettor: 4/18 mm Dell'Orto
Maximum power: 29.8 bhp
(DIN) at 10 500 rpm
Starting: electric

Transmission: 5-speed with
chain-drive

Electrics: 12 v coil ignition
with 12 Ah battery

Frame: Duplex tubular cradle

Suspension: Telescopic front
fork and rear adjustable
hydraulic shocks

Manufacturer: F.lli Benelli S.p.A.

Brakes: 260 mm single front
disc and 158 mm rear drum

Tyres: Front is 2.75–18
Rear is 3.00–18

Dimensions:
Length: 1 940 mm
Width: 711 mm
Wheelbase: 1 270 mm
Clearance: 203 mm
Seat height: 760 mm
Dry weight: 125 kg
Fuel tank: 12 litres

Performance:
Top speed: 150 km/h
Fuel consumption: 5.3 l/100 km

Features: Unique 4 cylinder
250.

BENELLI (Italy)

Model: Laser 50

Engine: 2-str disc valve single
Capacity: 49.6 cc
Bore × Stroke: 40 × 39.5 mm
Compression ratio: 9:1
Carburettor: 12 mm Dell'Orto
Maximum power: 1.5 bhp
(DIN)
Starting: kick

Transmission: 2-speed with
automatic drive

Electrics: Flywheel magneto
6 v ignition

Frame: Duplex tubular cradle

Suspension: Leading axle
front fork with rear monoshock
system

Manufacturer: F.lli Benelli S.p.A.

Brakes: 90 mm front drum
and 124 mm rear drum

Tyres: 3.00–10,
front and rear

Dimensions:
Length: 1 730 mm
Width: ...
Wheelbase: 1 230 mm
Clearance: ...
Seat height: ...
Dry weight: 51 kg
Fuel tank: 3.5 litres

Performance:
Top speed: 40 km/h
Fuel consumption: 1.9 l/100
km

Features: ...

BETA (Italy)

Model: KR 250

Engine: 2-str LC reed valve single
Capacity: 239 cc
Bore × Stroke: 72.8 × 57.5 mm
Compression ratio: ...
Carburettor: 25 mm Dell'Orto
Maximum power: ...
Starting: kick

Transmission: 6-speed with chain drive

Electrics: Transistorised 6 v ignition

Frame: Box section cradle

Suspension: Leading axle front fork and adjustable *Beta Monoshock* system

Brakes: 230 mm front disc and rear drum

Tyres: Front is 3.00–21
Rear is 4.00–18

Dimensions:
Length: ...
Width: ...
Wheelbase: 1 370 mm
Clearance: ...
Seat height: 845 mm
Dry weight: 104 kg
Fuel tank: 10 litres

Performance:
Top speed: 140 km/h
Fuel consumption: ...

Features: Also made in 125 cc version.

Manufacturer: Betamotor S.p.A., via Roma, 50067 Rignano Sull'Arno (Fi), Italy.

BIMOTA (Italy)

Model: SB5

Engine: 4-str Suzuki dohc four
Capacity: 1 135 cc
Bore × Stroke: 74 × 66 mm
Compression ratio: 9.7:1
Carburettor: 4/33 mm Mikuni
Maximum power: 115 bhp
(DIN) at 8 500 rpm
Starting: electric

Transmission: 5-speed with chain drive

Electrics: Transistorised 12 v ignition with 14 Ah battery

Frame: Chrome-moly tubing

Suspension: Telehydraulic fork with rear adjustable monoshock system

Brakes: 280 mm Brembo triple disc system

Tyres: Front is 120/80VR–16
Rear is 150/80VR–16 (Radials)

Dimensions:
Length: 2 100 mm
Width: 680 mm
Wheelbase: 1 455 mm
Clearance: 165 mm
Seat height: 800 mm
Dry weight: 215 kg
Fuel tank: 22 litres

Performance:
Top speed: 260 km/h
Fuel consumption: 5.8 l/100 km

Features: First two seater made and homologated by Bimota.

Manufacturer: Bimota S.p.A., via Giaccaglia 38, 47037 Rimini, Italy.

BIMOTA (Italy)

Model: SB4

Engine: 4-str Suzuki dohc four
Capacity: 1 074.9 cc
Bore × Stroke: 72 × 66 mm
Compression ratio: 9.5:1
Carburettor: 4/34 mm Mikuni
Maximum power: 112 bhp
(DIN) at 8 750 rpm
Starting: electric

Transmission: 5-speed with chain drive

Electrics: Transistorised 12 v ignition with 14 Ah battery

Frame: Chrome-moly tubing

Suspension: Telehydraulic fork with rear adjustable monoshock system

Brakes: 280 mm Brembo triple disc system

Tyres: Front is 120/80V–16
Rear is 150/80V–16 (Tubeless)

Dimensions:
Length: 2 115 mm
Width: 680 mm
Wheelbase: 1 435 mm
Clearance: 165 mm
Seat height: 760 mm
Dry weight: 212 kg
Fuel tank: 22 litres

Performance:
Top speed: 255 km/h
Fuel consumption: 5.6 l/100 km

Features: HB3 is a 115 bhp model with Honda CB1100F engine.

Manufacturer: Bimota S.p.A.

BMW (West Germany)

Model: K100RS

Engine: 4-str LC flat in-line four
Capacity: 988 cc
Bore × Stroke: 70 × 67 mm
Compression ratio: 10.2:1
Carburettor: fuel injection
Maximum power: 90 bhp (DIN) at 8 000 rpm
Starting: electric

Transmission: 5-speed with shaft drive

Electrics: Transistorised 12 v ignition with 20 Ah battery

Frame: Latticed tube

Suspension: Telehydraulic front fork and *Monolever* swinging arm with *Monoshock*

Brakes: 285 mm triple disc system with d-pc at the front

Tyres: Front is 100/90V–18
Rear is 130/90V–17 (Tubeless)

Dimensions:
Length: 2 200 mm
Width: 800 mm
Wheelbase: 1 516 mm
Clearance: 175 mm
Seat height: 810 mm
Dry weight: 229 kg
Fuel tank: 22 litres

Performance:
Top speed: 220 km/h
Fuel consumption: 5.7 l/100 km

Features: Compact drive system, LE Jetronic fuel injection, sports fairing.

Manufacturer: BMW Motorrad GmbH, 8000 München 45, West Germany.

BMW (West Germany)

Model: K100RT

Engine: 4-str LC flat in-line
four
Capacity: 988 cc
Bore × Stroke: 70 × 67 mm
Compression ratio: 10.2:1
Carburettor: fuel injection
Maximum power: 90 bhp
(DIN) at 8 000 rpm
Starting: electric

Transmission: 5-speed with
shaft drive

Electrics: Transistorised 12 v
ignition with 20 Ah battery

Frame: Latticed tube

Suspension: Telehydraulic
front fork and *Monolever*
swinging arm with *Monoshock*

Brakes: 285 mm triple disc
system with d-pc at the front

Tyres: Front is 100/90V–18
Rear is 130/90V–17 (Tubeless)

Dimensions:
Length: 2 200 mm
Width: 916 mm
Wheelbase: 1 516 mm
Clearance: 175 mm
Seat height: 810 mm
Dry weight: 239 kg
Fuel tank: 22 litres

Performance:
Top speed: 215 km/h
Fuel consumption: 5.91 l/100 km

Features: Touring fairing with
storage compartments.

Manufacturer: BMW Motorrad GmbH.

BMW (West Germany)

Model: R80RT

Engine: 4-str horizontally
opposed twin
Capacity: 797.5 cc
Bore × Stroke: 84 × 70.6 mm
Compression ratio: 8.2:1
Carburettor: 2/32 mm Bing
Maximum power: 50 bhp
(DIN) at 6 500 rpm
Starting: electric

Transmission: 5-speed with
shaft drive

Electrics: Transistorised 12 v
ignition with 20 Ah battery

Frame: Duplex tubular cradle

Suspension: Telescopic front
fork and rear *Monolever* with
adjustable *Monoshock*

Brakes: 285 mm single front
disc and 200 mm rear drum

Tyres: Front is 90/90H–18
Rear is 120/90H–18

Dimensions:
Length: 2 175 mm
Width: 960 mm
Wheelbase: 1 465 mm
Clearance: 140 mm
Seat height: 807 mm
Dry weight: 214 kg
Fuel tank: 22 litres

Performance:
Top speed: 170 km/h
Fuel consumption: 5.9 l/100 km

Features: Range includes R80
without fairing and R80ST, a
road version of the R80G/S.

Manufacturer: BMW Motorrad GmbH.

BMW (West Germany)

Model: R80G/S Paris–Dakar

Engine: 4-str horizontally opposed twin
Capacity: 798 cc
Bore × Stroke: 84 × 70.6 mm
Compression ratio: 8:1
Carburettor: 2/32 mm Bing
Maximum power: 50 bhp (DIN) at 6 500 rpm
Starting: electric/kick

Transmission: 5-speed with shaft drive

Electrics: Transistorised 12 v ignition with 20 Ah battery

Frame: Duplex tubular cradle

Suspension: Telescopic front fork and rear *Monolever* with adjustable *Monoshock*

Brakes: 285 mm single front disc and 200 mm rear drum

Tyres: Front is 3.00–21
Rear is 4.00–18

Dimensions:
Length: 2 230 mm
Width: 746 mm
Wheelbase: 1 485 mm
Clearance: . . .
Seat height: 875 mm
Dry weight: 185 kg
Fuel tank: 32 litres

Performance:
Top speed: 168 km/h
Fuel consumption: 5.5 l/100 km

Features: Modelled on Gaston Rahier's winning bike in the 1984 Paris–Dakar Rally.

Manufacturer: BMW Motorrad GmbH.

BMW (West Germany)

Model: R65LS

Engine: 4-str horizontally opposed twin
Capacity: 650 cc
Bore × Stroke: 82 × 61.5 mm
Compression ratio: 9.2:1
Carburettor: 2/32 mm Bing
Maximum power: 50 bhp (DIN) at 7 250 rpm
Starting: electric

Transmission: 5-speed with shaft drive

Electrics: Transistorised 12 v ignition with 20 Ah battery

Frame: Duplex tubular cradle

Suspension: Telescopic front fork and rear *Monolever* with adjustable *Monoshock*

Brakes: Twin 285 mm front discs and rear 200 mm drum

Tyres: Front is 3.25–18
Rear is 4.00–18

Dimensions:
Length: 2 110 mm
Width: 688 mm
Wheelbase: 1 400 mm
Clearance: 139 mm
Seat height: 810 mm
Dry weight: 185 kg
Fuel tank: 22 litres

Performance:
Top speed: 175 km/h
Fuel consumption: 4.6 l/100 km

Features: Boxer series also includes the unfaired R65 and the smaller R45.

Manufacturer: BMW Motorrad GmbH.

BOMBARDIER CAN-AM (Canada)

Model: 500 ASE

Engine: 2-str rotary valve
Rotax single
Capacity: 482.3 cc
Bore × Stroke: 85 × 85 mm
Compression ratio: ...
Carburettor: 40 mm Bing
Maximum power: 50 bhp
Starting: kick

Transmission: 5-speed with
chain drive

Electrics: Bosch CDI 6 v
ignition

Frame: Reynolds 531 tubing

Suspension: Leading axle
front fork with rear *Quad
Link II* monoshock system

Brakes: 140 mm drums at
front and rear

Tyres: Front is 3.00–21
Rear is 5.10–18

Dimensions:
Length: ...
Width: ...
Wheelbase: 1 511 mm
Clearance: 355 mm
Seat height: 965 mm
Dry weight: 111.5 kg
Fuel tank: 13.6 litres

Performance:
Top speed: ...
Fuel consumption: ...

Features: Enduro lighting,
spark arrestor, quick detach rear
wheel, kickstand.

Manufacturer: Bombardier Inc, Valcourt, Quebec,
Canada JOE 2LO.

BOMBARDIER CAN-AM (Canada)

Model: 250 ASE L/C

Engine: 2-str LC rotary valve
single
Capacity: 248 cc
Bore × Stroke: 72 × 61 mm
Compression ratio: 13:1
Carburettor: 34 mm Mikuni
Maximum power: 35 bhp
Starting: kick

Transmission: 6-speed with
chain drive

Electrics: Bosch CDI 6 v
ignition

Frame: Reynolds 531 tubing

Suspension: Leading axle
front fork with rear *Quad
Link II* monoshock system

Manufacturer: Bombardier Inc.

Brakes: 140 mm drums at
front and rear

Tyres: Front is 3.00–21
Rear is 4.50–18

Dimensions:
Length: ...
Width: ...
Wheelbase: 1 511 mm
Clearance: 375 mm
Seat height: 965 mm
Dry weight: 101 kg
Fuel tank: 10.45 litres

Performance:
Top speed: ...
Fuel consumption: ...

Features: Rotax automatic
variable exhaust system
(RAVE). Range also includes
200 ASE.

BSA (UK)

Model: 125 Tracker

Engine: 2-str reed valve single
Capacity: 123 cc
Bore × Stroke: 56 × 50 mm
Compression ratio: 7:1
Carburettor: 22 mm Mikuni
Maximum power: 12 bhp
(DIN) at 7 000 rpm
Starting: kick

Transmission: 6-speed with
chain drive

Electrics: Flywheel magneto
6 v ignition with 4 Ah battery

Frame: Tubular cradle

Suspension: Telescopic front
fork with rear monoshock
system

Brakes: 160 mm front drum
and 140 mm rear drum

Tyres: Front is 2.75–21
Rear is 3.50–18

Dimensions:
Length: 2 000 mm
Width: 899 mm
Wheelbase: 1 320 mm
Clearance: 240 mm
Seat height: 750 mm
Dry weight: 94 kg
Fuel tank: 4.6 litres

Performance:
Top speed: 105 km/h
Fuel consumption: 4 l/100 km

Features: Also as 175 cc
model with front disc brake.

Manufacturer: BSA Company Ltd., Bannerley Road, Garretts
Green, Birmingham B33 0SH, England.

BULTACO (Spain)

Model: Alpina

Engine: 2-str piston port
single
Capacity: 237.5 cc
Bore × Stroke: 71 × 60 mm
Compression ratio: 9:1
Carburettor: 27 mm Amal
Maximum power: 14.1 bhp
(DIN) at 5 500 rpm
Starting: kick

Transmission: 5-speed with
chain drive

Electrics: Flywheel magneto
6 v ignition and 8 Ah battery

Frame: Tubular single cradle

Suspension: Telescopic front
fork with twin rear hydraulic
shocks

Brakes: 140 mm drums at
front and rear

Tyres: Front is 2.75–21
Rear is 4.00–18

Dimensions:
Length: 2 002 mm
Width: 830 mm
Wheelbase: 1 310 mm
Clearance: 300 mm
Seat height: 820 mm
Dry weight: 105 kg
Fuel tank: 8.5 litres

Performance:
Top speed: ...
Fuel consumption: ...

Features: Also as a 350 cc
model.

Manufacturer: Bultaco Compañia Española de Motores S.A., San
Adrian de Besós E-1047, Barcelona, Spain.

CAGIVA (Italy)

Model: Ala Azzurra 650

Engine: 4-str sohc 90° Desmo
vee twin
Capacity: 649.5 cc
Bore × Stroke: 82 × 61.5 mm
Compression ratio: 10:1
Carburettor: 2/36 mm Dell'Orto
Maximum power: 47 bhp
(DIN) at 8 250 rpm
Starting: electric

Transmission: 5-speed with
chain drive

Electrics: Transistorised 12 v
ignition and 36 Ah battery

Frame: Duplex tubular cradle

Suspension: Telehydraulic
front fork with 5-way
adjustable *Koni* shocks

Brakes: 260 mm triple disc
system

Tyres: Front is 100/90H–18
Rear is 110/90H–18

Dimensions:
Length: 2 160 mm
Width: 710 mm
Wheelbase: 1 450 mm
Clearance: 175 mm
Seat height: 800 mm
Dry weight: 183.5 kg
Fuel tank: 20 litres

Performance:
Top speed: 185 km/h
Fuel consumption: 6 l/100 km

Features: Ducati built Pantah
engine. Also built with 350 cc
engine.

Manufacturer: Cagiva Motor Italia S.p.A.

CAGIVA (Italy)

Model: Aletta Electra 125

Engine: 2-str rotary disc valve single
Capacity: 123.15 cc
Bore × Stroke: 56 × 50 mm
Compression ratio: 11.9:1
Carburettor: 24 mm Dell'Orto
Maximum power: 13.5 bhp (DIN) at 7 250 rpm
Starting: electric/kick

Transmission: 6-speed with chain drive

Electrics: Transistorised 12 v Motoplat ignition

Frame: Duplex tubular cradle

Suspension: Telehydraulic front fork with rear adjustable *Soft Damp* system

Brakes: 260 mm front disc and rear 140 mm drum

Tyres: Front is 3.00–18
Rear is 3.50–18

Dimensions:
Length: ...
Width: ...
Wheelbase: 1 360 mm
Clearance: ...
Seat height: 810 mm
Dry weight: 120 kg
Fuel tank: 10.5 litres

Performance:
Top speed: 113 km/h
Fuel consumption: 4.7 l/100 km

Features: ...

Manufacturer: Cagiva Motor Italia S.p.A., via G. Macchi 144, 21100 Varese (Schiranna), Italy.

CASAL (Portugal)

Model: K276

Engine: 2-str piston port single
Capacity: 123.7 cc
Bore × Stroke: 54 × 54 mm
Compression ratio: 10:1
Carburettor: 26 mm Bing
Maximum power: 14 bhp (DIN) at 6 500 rpm
Starting: kick

Transmission: 6-speed with chain drive

Electrics: Transistorised 6 v Motoplat ignition

Frame: Duplex tubular cradle

Suspension: Telescopic front fork with twin rear hydraulic shocks

Brakes: 140 mm front drum and 160 mm rear drum

Tyres: Front is 2.75–21
Rear is 3.50–18

Dimensions:
Length: 2 020 mm
Width: 830 mm
Wheelbase: 1 330 mm
Clearance: ...
Seat height: 830 mm
Dry weight: 107 kg
Fuel tank: 9 litres

Performance:
Top speed: 120 km/h
Fuel consumption: 4.5 l/100 km

Features: ...

Manufacturer: Metalurgia Casal S.A.R.L., Apartado 83, 3801 Aveiro, Portugal.

CASAL (Portugal)

Model: K551

Engine: 2-str piston port single
Capacity: 49.9 cc
Bore × Stroke: 40 × 39.7 mm
Compression ratio: 8.5:1
Carburettor: 19 mm Bing
Maximum power: 7.3 bhp (DIN) at 8 500 rpm
Starting: kick

Transmission: 6-speed with chain drive

Electrics: Flywheel magneto 6 v ignition

Frame: Duplex tubular cradle

Suspension: Telescopic front fork with twin rear hydraulic shocks

Brakes: 220 mm front disc with 118 mm rear drum

Tyres: Front is 2.50–17
Rear is 2.75–17

Dimensions:
Length: 1 840 mm
Width: 730 mm
Wheelbase: 1 240 mm
Clearance: ...
Seat height: 790 mm
Dry weight: 82 kg
Fuel tank: 12 litres

Performance:
Top speed: 98 km/h
Fuel consumption: 3.2 l/100 km

Features: Casal range includes K168, K177, K180, K181 and the liquid cooled RZ50.

Manufacturer: Metalurgia Casal S.A.R.L.

CASAL (Portugal)

Model: K506

Engine: 2-str piston port single
Capacity: 49.9 cc
Bore × Stroke: 40 × 39.7 mm
Compression ratio: 8.5:1
Carburettor: 19 mm Bing
Maximum power: 7.3 bhp (DIN) at 8 500 rpm
Starting: kick

Transmission: 6-speed with chain drive

Electrics: Flywheel magneto 6 v ignition

Frame: Duplex tubular cradle

Suspension: Telescopic front fork with twin rear hydraulic shocks

Brakes: 140 mm drums at front and rear

Tyres: Front is 2.75–21
Rear is 3.00–18

Dimensions:
Length: 2 030 mm
Width: 910 mm
Wheelbase: 1 350 mm
Clearance: ...
Seat height: 900 mm
Dry weight: 80 kg
Fuel tank: 6 litres

Performance:
Top speed: 98 km/h
Fuel consumption: 3.2 l/100 km

Features: Range includes a 125 cc version.

Manufacturer: Metalurgia Casal S.A.R.L.

CZ (Czechoslovakia)

Model: Type 487

Engine: 2-str piston port single
Capacity: 172 cc
Bore × Stroke: 58 × 65 mm
Compression ratio: 8.6:1
Carburettor: 26 mm Jikov
Maximum power: 15 bhp (DIN) at 5 500 rpm
Starting: kick

Transmission: 4-speed with chain drive

Electrics: 6 v coil ignition with 14 Ah battery

Frame: Duplex tubular cradle

Suspension: Telescopic front fork with 4-way adjustable rear hydraulic shocks

Brakes: 160 mm drums at front and rear

Tyres: Front is 2.75–18
Rear is 3.00–18

Dimensions:
Length: 2 010 mm
Width: 715 mm
Wheelbase: 1 320 mm
Clearance: 125 mm
Seat height: 800 mm
Dry weight: 120 kg
Fuel tank: 13 litres

Performance:
Top speed: 100 km/h
Fuel consumption: 3.8 l/100 km

Features: Range includes the Types 472 (350 cc) and 488 (125 cc).

Manufacturer: České Závody Motocyklové Strakonice,

DUCATI (Italy)

Model: Replica Desmo

Engine: 4-str sohc 90° vee-twin
Capacity: 973 cc
Bore × Stroke: 88 × 80 mm
Compression ratio: 9.5:1
Carburettor: 2/40 mm Dell'Orto
Maximum power: 90 bhp
(DIN) at 7 500 rpm
Starting: electric

Transmission: 5-speed with chain drive

Electrics: Transistorised 12 v ignition with 12 Ah battery

Frame: Duplex tubular cradle

Suspension: Telehydraulic front fork with adjustable twin rear shocks

Brakes: 280 mm triple disc system

Tyres: Front is 100/90V–18
Rear is 130/80V–18

Dimensions:
Length: 2 220 mm
Width: 675 mm
Wheelbase: 1 500 mm
Clearance: 158 mm
Seat height: 770 mm
Dry weight: 198 kg
Fuel tank: 18 litres

Performance:
Top speed: 220 km/h
Fuel consumption: 6 l/100 km

Features: Replica of the bike on which the late Mike Hailwood MBE won his 10th and final TT Championship.

Manufacturer: Ducati Meccanica S.p.A., via A. Cavalieri Ducati 3, 40132 Bologna, Italy.

ENFIELD (India)

Model: 350 Bullet

Engine: 4-str ohv single
Capacity: 346 cc
Bore × Stroke: 70 × 90 mm
Compression ratio: 7.25:1
Carburettor: 26 mm Bing
Maximum power: 18 bhp
(DIN) at 5 650 rpm
Starting: kick

Transmission: 4-speed with
chain drive

Electrics: 6 v coil ignition and
12 Ah battery

Frame: Single tubular cradle

Suspension: Telescopic front
fork with twin rear hydraulic
shocks

Brakes: 150 mm drums front
and rear

Tyres: 3.25–19 front and at
rear

Dimensions:
Length: 2 120 mm
Width: ...
Wheelbase: 1 372 mm
Clearance: 140 mm
Seat height: 875 mm
Dry weight: 163 kg
Fuel tank: 15 litres

Performance:
Top speed: 120 km/h
Fuel consumption: 4 l/100 km

Features: ...

Manufacturer: Enfield India Ltd., Po 5284, Tiruvottiyur, Madras
600 019, India.

FANTIC (Italy)

Model: 125 Sport HP1

Engine: 2-str LC 4 transfer
ports single
Capacity: 124.4 cc
Bore × Stroke: 55.2 × 52 mm
Compression ratio: 12:1
Carburettor: 26 mm Dell'Orto
Maximum power: 25 bhp
(SAE) at 8 250 rpm
Starting: kick

Transmission: 6-speed with
chain drive

Electrics: Transistorised 12 v
ignition and 4 Ah battery

Frame: Box section cradle

Suspension: Telehydraulic
front fork with anti-dive and
rear *Single Shock System*

Manufacturer: Fanticmotor S.p.A.

Brakes: Twin 240 mm front
discs and 160 mm rear drum

Tyres: Front is 3.25–16R
Rear is 3.25S–18

Dimensions:
Length: ...
Width: ...
Wheelbase: ...
Clearance: ...
Seat height: ...
Dry weight: ...
Fuel tank: 12.5 litres

Performance:
Top speed: 140 km/h
Fuel consumption: 4.7 l/100 km

Features: ...

FANTIC (Italy)

Model: Raider 50

Engine: 2-str LC 4 transfer ports single
Capacity: 49.6 cc
Bore × Stroke: 38.8 × 42 mm
Compression ratio: 11:1
Carburettor: 12 mm Dell'Orto
Maximum power: 1.5 bhp
Starting: kick

Transmission: 4-speed with chain drive

Electrics: Transistorised 12 v ignition and 4 Ah battery

Frame: Duplex tubular cradle

Suspension: Telehydraulic leading link fork with rear *Single Shock System*

Brakes: 220 mm front disc and 118 mm rear drum

Tyres: Front is 2.75–21
Rear is 4.10–18

Dimensions:
Length: ...
Width: ...
Wheelbase: 1 350 mm
Clearance: ...
Seat height: ...
Dry weight: 87 kg
Fuel tank: 8.5 litres

Performance:
Top speed: 48 km/h
Fuel consumption: 2.2 l/100 km

Features: Series includes 18 bhp 125 cc and a 25 bhp 250 cc.

Manufacturer: Fanticmotor S.p.A., via Parini 3, 22061 Barzago (CO), Italy.

GARELLI (Italy)

Model: GTA 125

Engine: 2-str LC reed valve
single
Capacity: 124.8 cc
Bore × Stroke: 52.8 × 57 mm
Compression ratio: 14.5:1
Carburettor: 28 mm Dell'Orto
Maximum power: 22 bhp
(DIN) at 8 250 rpm
Starting: electric

Transmission: 6-speed with
chain drive

Electrics: Transistorised 12 v
ignition with 9 Ah battery

Frame: Box section cradle

Suspension: Telehydraulic
front fork with anti-dive and
rear *Soft lever* system

Brakes: 240 mm front disc
and 160 mm rear drum

Tyres: Front is 3.25–16
Rear is 3.50–18

Dimensions:
Length: 2 000 mm
Width: 570 mm
Wheelbase: 1 340 mm
Clearance: ...
Seat height: ...
Dry weight: 110 kg
Fuel tank: 15 litres

Performance:
Top speed: 130 km/h
Fuel consumption: 3.3 l/100 km

Features: ...

Manufacturer: Agrati Garelli S.p.A., via Immacolata 25,
22068 Monticello Brianzo (Como), Italy.

GARELLI (Italy)

Model: Tiger 125XRD

Engine: 2-str LC reed valve single
Capacity: 124.8 cc
Bore × Stroke: 52.8 × 57 mm
Compression ratio: 14.5:1
Carburettor: 28 mm Dell'Orto
Maximum power: 21 bhp (DIN) at 8 000 rpm
Starting: kick

Transmission: 6-speed with chain drive

Electrics: Transistorised 12 v ignition with 5 Ah battery

Frame: Box section cradle

Suspension: Telehydraulic front fork with rear *Soft lever* monoshock system

Manufacturer: Agrati Garelli S.p.A.

Brakes: 230 mm front disc and 125 mm rear drum

Tyres: Front is 2.75–21
Rear is 4.10–18

Dimensions:
Length: 2 140 mm
Width: 900 mm
Wheelbase: 1 370 mm
Clearance: . . .
Seat height: 880 mm
Dry weight: 115 kg
Fuel tank: 18 litres

Performance:
Top speed: 120 km/h
Fuel consumption: 3.5 l/100 km

Features: XR model has a 12 litre tank.

GARELLI (Italy)

Model: TSR 125

Engine: 2-str LC piston port
single
Capacity: 123.5 cc
Bore × Stroke: 55 × 52 mm
Compression ratio: 10:1
Carburettor: 26 mm Dell'Orto
Maximum power: 16 bhp
(DIN) at 7 000 rpm
Starting: kick

Transmission: 5-speed with
chain drive

Electrics: Transistorised 12 v
ignition with 7 Ah battery

Frame: Duplex tubular cradle

Suspension: Telehydraulic
front fork and rear 5-way
adjustable hydraulic shocks

Manufacturer: Agrati Garelli S.p.A.

Brakes: 260 mm front disc
and 160 mm rear drum

Tyres: Front is 2.75–18
Rear is 3.25–18

Dimensions:
Length: 2 000 mm
Width: 810 mm
Wheelbase: 1 330 mm
Clearance: ...
Seat height: ...
Dry weight: 115 kg
Fuel tank: 11 litres

Performance:
Top speed: 110 km/h
Fuel consumption: 3.2 l/100 km

Features: ...

GARELLI (Italy)

Model: Ciclone LC

Engine: 2-str LC piston port single
Capacity: 49.6 cc
Bore × Stroke: 40 × 39.5 mm
Compression ratio: 9:1
Carburettor: 12 mm Dell'Orto
Maximum power: 1.5 bhp (DIN) at 5 000 rpm
Starting: kick

Transmission: 5-speed with chain drive

Electrics: Flywheel magneto ignition

Frame: Step-thru

Suspension: Telescopic front fork and rear 3-way adjustable hydraulic shocks

Manufacturer: Agrati Garelli S.p.A.

Brakes: 220 mm front disc and 118 mm rear drum

Tyres: Front is 2.50–17
Rear is 3.25–16

Dimensions:
Length: 1 760 mm
Width: 780 mm
Wheelbase: 1 200 mm
Clearance: . . .
Seat height: . . .
Dry weight: 64 kg
Fuel tank: 3.4 litres

Performance:
Top speed: 40 km/h
Fuel consumption: 2 l/100 km

Features: Other Garelli mopeds include the VIP and Noi series.

GILERA (Italy)

Model: RV200

Engine: 2-str LC rotary valve single
Capacity: 183.4 cc
Bore × Stroke: ...
Compression ratio: 13.5:1
Carburettor: 26 mm Dell'Orto
Maximum power: 25 bhp (DIN) at 7 750 rpm
Starting: electric

Transmission: 6-speed with chain drive

Electrics: Transistorised 12 v ignition

Frame: Duplex tubular cradle

Suspension: Telehydraulic front fork with anti-dive and rear *Monodrive* system

Brakes: 240 mm discs front and rear

Tyres: Front is 100/90–16
Rear is 110/90–18

Dimensions:
Length: ...
Width: ...
Wheelbase: 1 350 mm
Clearance: ...
Seat height: ...
Dry weight: ...
Fuel tank: 20 litres

Performance:
Top speed: 138 km/h
Fuel consumption: ...

Features: Other RV models include RV250NGR and RV125. Also in motocross styling.

Manufacturer: Gilera-Piaggio S.p.A., via C. Battisti 68, 20043 Arcore (MI), Italy.

GILERA (Italy)

Model: RX125 Arizona

Engine: 2-str LC rotary valve
single
Capacity: 124.3 cc
Bore × Stroke: 58 × 50.5 mm
Compression ratio: ...
Carburettor: 26 mm Dell'Orto
Maximum power: 19 bhp
(DIN) at 7 750 rpm
Starting: kick

Transmission: 6-speed with
chain drive

Electrics: Transistorised 12 v
ignition

Frame: Duplex tubular cradle

Suspension: Leading axle
front fork with rear adjustable
Monodrive system

Brakes: 230 mm front disc
and 140 mm rear drum

Tyres: Front is 2.75–21
Rear is 4.10–18

Dimensions:
Length: ...
Width: ...
Wheelbase: ...
Clearance: ...
Seat height: ...
Dry weight: 118 kg
Fuel tank: 22 litres

Performance:
Top speed: 115 km/h
Fuel consumption: ...

Features: RX125 has a 13
litre fuel tank.

Manufacturer: Gilera-Piaggio S.p.A.

GILERA (Italy)

Model: GSA Superstart

Engine: 2-str fan-cooled single
Capacity: 49.77 cc
Bore × Stroke: 38.4 × 43 mm
Compression ratio: 9.5:1
Carburettor: 12 mm Dell'Orto
Maximum power: 1.5 bhp (DIN) at 4 800 rpm
Starting: electric/kick

Transmission: Variable speed automatic with belt drive

Electrics: Transistorised 6 v ignition

Frame: Monocoque

Suspension: Telescopic front fork with rear side shock and coaxial spring

Manufacturer: Gilera-Piaggio S.p.A.

Brakes: Drums front and rear

Tyres: 3.50–10 at front and rear

Dimensions:
Length: 1 650 mm
Width: 640 mm
Wheelbase: 1 180 mm
Clearance: . . .
Seat height: . . .
Dry weight: 73 kg
Fuel tank: 4.2 litres

Performance:
Top speed: 40 km/h
Fuel consumption: 1.8 l/100 km

Features: Basic version is 50 GSA.

GILERA (Italy)

Model: CBA

Engine: 2-str piston port
single
Capacity: 49.28 cc
Bore × Stroke: 38.2 × 43 mm
Compression ratio: 9:1
Carburettor: 12 mm Dell'Orto
Maximum power: 1.5 bhp
(DIN) at 4 500 rpm
Starting: pedal

Transmission: Variable speed
automatic

Electrics: Flywheel magneto
6 v ignition

Frame: Step-thru

Suspension: Telescopic front
fork with twin rear hydraulic
shocks

Brakes: 104 mm drums at
front and rear

Tyres: 2.50–16 front and rear

Dimensions:
Length: 1 720 mm
Width: ...
Wheelbase: 1 164 mm
Clearance: ...
Seat height: ...
Dry weight: 55 kg
Fuel tank: 4.7 litres

Performance:
Top speed: 39 km/h
Fuel consumption: 1.9 l/100 km

Features: CBI is a 4-speed
version with kick start.

Manufacturer: Gilera-Piaggio S.p.A.

HARLEY-DAVIDSON (USA)

Model: Electra Glide FLHT

Engine: 4-str ohv 45° vee-twin
Capacity: 1 340 cc
Bore × Stroke: 88.8 × 108 mm
Compression ratio: 8.5:1
Carburettor: 38 mm Keihin
Maximum power: 70 bhp
(DIN) at 5 500 rpm
Starting: electric

Transmission: 5-speed with
Polychain belt drive

Electrics: Transistorised 12 v
ignition with 19 Ah battery

Frame: Duplex tubular cradle

Suspension: Air-assisted fork
with anti-dive and rear air-
adjustable shocks

Brakes: Twin 292 mm front
discs and 305 mm rear disc

Tyres: MT 90–16T front and
rear

Dimensions:
Length: 2 394 mm
Width: ...
Wheelbase: 1 599 mm
Clearance: 130 mm
Seat height: 711 mm
Dry weight: 323 kg
Fuel tank: 19 litres

Performance:
Top speed: 165 km/h
Fuel consumption: 5 l/100 km

Features: Tour Glide FLT
similar with larger handlebar
fairing.

Manufacturer: Harley-Davidson International, 689 Hope Street,
P.O. Box 4900 Stamford, Connecticut 06907–0900, USA.

HARLEY-DAVIDSON (USA)

Model: Sport Glide FXRT

Engine: 4-str ohv 45° vee-twin
Capacity: 1 340 cc
Bore × Stroke: 88.8 × 108 mm
Compression ratio: 8.5:1
Carburettor: 38 mm Keihin
Maximum power: 69 bhp
(DIN) at 5 500 rpm
Starting: electric

Transmission: 5-speed with
Polychain belt drive

Electrics: Transistorised 12 v
ignition with 19 Ah battery

Frame: Duplex tubular cradle

Suspension: Air-assisted fork
with anti-dive and rear air-
adjustable shocks

Brakes: 292 mm triple disc
system

Tyres: Front is MM90–19
Rear is MT90–16

Dimensions:
Length: 2 398 mm
Width: 863 mm
Wheelbase: 1 643 mm
Clearance: 155 mm
Seat height: 699 mm
Dry weight: 290 kg
Fuel tank: 15.9 litres

Performance:
Top speed: 165 km/h
Fuel consumption: 5 l/100 km

Features: Other Harley models
include the Wide Glide FXWG
and the Low Glide FXRS.

Manufacturer: Harley-Davidson International.

HARLEY DAVIDSON (USA)

Model: Soft Tail FXST

Engine: 4-str ohv 45° vee-twin
Capacity: 1340 cc
Bore × Stroke: 88.8 × 108 mm
Compression ratio: 8.5:1
Carburettor: 38 mm Keihin
Maximum power: 67 bhp
(DIN) at 5 500 rpm
Starting: electric/kick

Transmission: 4-speed with
chain drive

Electrics: Transistorised 12 v
ignition with 19 Ah battery

Frame: Duplex tubular cradle

Suspension: Telescopic front
forks with twin rear adjustable
shocks

Brakes: 292 mm discs at front
and rear

Tyres: Front is MH90–21
Rear is MT90–16

Dimensions:
Length: 2 395 mm
Width: ...
Wheelbase: 1 684 mm
Clearance: 152 mm
Seat height: 663 mm
Dry weight: 280 kg
Fuel tank: 19.7 litres

Performance:
Top speed: 180 km/h
Fuel consumption: 4 l/100 km

Features: Basic Harley model
is the Fat-Bob FXEF.

Manufacturer: Harley-Davidson International.

HARLEY-DAVIDSON (USA)

Model: Low Rider FXSB

Engine: 4-str ohv 45° vee-twin
Capacity: 1 340 cc
Bore × Stroke: 88.8 × 108 mm
Compression ratio: 8.5:1
Carburettor: 38 mm Keihin
Maximum power: 63 bhp
(DIN) at 5 500 rpm
Starting: electric/kick

Transmission: 4-speed with
Polychain belt drive

Electrics: Transistorised 12 v
ignition with 19 Ah battery

Frame: Duplex tubular cradle

Suspension: Air-assisted fork
with air-adjustable twin rear
shocks

Brakes: 292 mm discs at front
and rear

Tyres: Front is MJ90–19
Rear is MT90–16

Dimensions:
Length: 2 337 mm
Width: ...
Wheelbase: 1 613 mm
Clearance: 146 mm
Seat height: 686 mm
Dry weight: 261 kg
Fuel tank: 15.9 litres

Performance:
Top speed: ...
Fuel consumption: ...

Features: ...

Manufacturer: Harley-Davidson International.

HARLEY-DAVIDSON (USA)

Model: Sportster XLH

Engine: 4-str ohv 45° vee-twin
Capacity: 998 cc
Bore × Stroke: 81 × 96.8 mm
Compression ratio: 8.8:1
Carburettor: 34 mm Dell'Orto
Maximum power: 62 bhp
(DIN) at 6 000 rpm
Starting: electric

Transmission: 4-speed with
chain drive

Electrics: Transistorised 12 v
ignition with 19 Ah battery

Frame: Duplex tubular cradle

Suspension: Telescopic front
fork with twin rear hydraulic
shocks

Brakes: 292 mm discs at front
and rear

Tyres: Front is MJ90–19
Rear is MT90–16

Dimensions:
Length: 2 223 mm
Width: ...
Wheelbase: 1 524 mm
Clearance: 170 mm
Seat height: 724 mm
Dry weight: 216 kg
Fuel tank: 8.5 litres

Performance:
Top speed: 180 km/h
Fuel consumption: 4 l/100 km

Features: The "small" Harley
models include the Roadster
XLS with cast wheels.

Manufacturer: Harley-Davidson International.

HARLEY-DAVIDSON (USA)

Model: XLX-61

Engine: 4-str ohv 45° vee-twin
Capacity: 998 cc
Bore × Stroke: 81 × 96.8 mm
Compression ratio: 8.8:1
Carburettor: 34 mm Dell'Orto
Maximum power: 62 bhp
(DIN) at 6 000 rpm
Starting: electric

Transmission: 4-speed with
chain drive

Electrics: Transistorised 12 v
ignition with 19 Ah battery

Frame: Duplex tubular cradle

Suspension: Telescopic front
fork with twin rear hydraulic
shocks

Brakes: 292 mm discs at front
and rear

Tyres: Front is MJ90–19
Rear is MT90–16

Dimensions:
Length: 2 223 mm
Width: ...
Wheelbase: 1 524 mm
Clearance: 170 mm
Seat height: 730 mm
Dry weight: 212 kg
Fuel tank: 8.5 litres

Performance:
Top speed: 200 km/h
Fuel consumption: 4 l/100 km

Features: ...

Manufacturer: Harley-Davidson International.

HESKETH (UK)

Model: V1000

Engine: 4-str dohc 90° 4-valve
vee-twin
Capacity: 992.3 cc
Bore × Stroke: 95 × 70 mm
Compression ratio: 10.5:1
Carburettor: 2/36 mm Dell'Orto
Maximum power: 86 bhp
(DIN) at 6 500 rpm
Starting: electric

Transmission: 5-speed with
chain drive

Electrics: Transistorised 12 v
ignition with 27 Ah battery

Frame: Duplex tubular cradle

Suspension: Telehydraulic
front fork with rear 3-way
adjustable hydraulic shocks

Brakes: 280 mm Brembo triple
disc system

Tyres: Front is 100/90V–19
Rear is 130/90V–17

Dimensions:
Length: 2 235 mm
Width: 712 mm
Wheelbase: 1 510 mm
Clearance: 140 mm
Seat height: 838 mm
Dry weight: 247 kg
Fuel tank: 23 litres

Performance:
Top speed: over 210 km/h
Fuel consumption: 6 l/100 km

Features: Vampire model has
full fairing. Both models
currently produced by Mocheck
Ltd., London SW4.

Manufacturer: Hesleydon Ltd., Eaton Neston, Towcester,
Northants, NN12 7HS, England.

HONDA (Japan)

Model: 1200A Gold Wing Aspencade

Engine: 4-str LC ohc opposed flat four
Capacity: 1 182 cc
Bore × Stroke: 75.5 × 66 mm
Compression ratio: 9:1
Carburettor: 4/32 mm cv Keihin
Maximum power: 94 bhp (DIN) at 7 000 rpm
Starting: electric

Transmission: 4-speed and overdrive with shaft drive

Electrics: Transistorised 12 v ignition with 20 Ah battery

Frame: Duplex tubular cradle

Suspension: Air-assisted fork with dual *TRAC* and rear air-assisted dampers

Brakes: Triple disc system in linked braking arrangement

Tyres: Front is 130/90H–16
Rear is 150/90H–15

Dimensions:
Length: 2 505 mm
Width: 970 mm
Wheelbase: 1 610 mm
Clearance: 140 mm
Seat height: 780 mm
Dry weight: 329 kg
Fuel tank: 22 litres

Performance:
Top speed: 175 km/h
Fuel consumption: 7 l/100 km

Features: Futuristic instrument control with LCD readouts. Radio and cassette system.
TRAC is Torque Reactive Anti-Dive Control to limit front fork dive on braking.

Manufacturer: Honda Motor Co. Ltd., 27–8, 6-chome, Jingumae, Shibuyaku, Tokyo, Japan,

HONDA (Japan)

Model: VF1000R

Engine: 4-str LC dohc
16-valve vee 4
Capacity: 998 cc
Bore × Stroke: 77 × 53.6 mm
Compression ratio: 11:1
Carburettor: 4/36 cm cv Keihin
Maximum power: 122 bhp
(DIN) at 10 000 rpm
Starting: electric

Transmission: 5-speed with
chain drive

Electrics: Transistorised 12 v
with electronic advance

Frame: Box section cradle

Suspension: Air-assisted front
fork with *TRAC* and 3-way
adjustable *Pro-Link*

Brakes: Twin floating front
discs with d-pc and rear disc

Tyres: Front is 120/80–16
Rear is 140/80V–17 (Radials)

Dimensions:
Length: 2 187 mm
Width: 735 mm
Wheelbase: 1 505 mm
Clearance: 135 mm
Seat height: 810 mm
Dry weight: 238 kg
Fuel tank: 25.5 litres

Performance:
Top speed: over 250 km/h
Fuel consumption: 7.8 l/100
km

Features: One-way clutch
mechanism. *TRAC* anti-dive
system. Endurance style dual
headlights.
headlights.

Manufacturer: Honda Motor Co. Ltd.

HONDA (Japan)

Model: VF1000F2 Bol D'or

Engine: 4-str LC dohc
16-valve vee 4
Capacity: 998 cc
Bore × Stroke: 77 × 53.6 mm
Compression ratio: 10.5:1
Carburettor: 4/36 mm cv Keihin
Maximum power: 116 bhp
(DIN) at 10 000 rpm
Starting: electric

Transmission: 5-speed with
chain drive

Electrics: Transistorised 12 v
with electronic advance

Frame: Box section cradle

Suspension: Air-assisted front
fork with *TRAC* and 3-way
adjustable *Pro-Link*

Brakes: Twin front discs with
d-pc and rear disc

Tyres: Front is 100/90V–18
Rear is 140/80V–17

Dimensions:
Length: 2 270 mm
Width: 750 mm
Wheelbase: 1 549 mm
Clearance: 140 mm
Seat height: 820 mm
Dry weight: 240 kg
Fuel tank: 23 litres

Performance:
Top speed: over 230 km/h
Fuel consumption: 7.8 l/100 km

Features: *TRAC* anti-dive
system. Cast aluminium
swinging arm. Dual headlights.
Based on VF1000F model.

Manufacturer: Honda Motor Co. Ltd.

HONDA (Japan)

Model: CBX750F-E

Engine: 4-str dohc 16-valve
in-line four
Capacity: 747 cc
Bore × Stroke: 67 × 53 mm
Compression ratio: 9.3:1
Carburettor: 4/36 mm cv Keihin
Maximum power: 91 bhp
(DIN) at 9500 rpm
Starting: electric

Transmission: 6-speed with
chain drive

Electrics: Transistorised 12 v
with electronic advance

Frame: Duplex tubular cradle

Suspension: Air-assisted front
fork with 3-way remote
adjustable *Pro-Link*

Brakes: Twin front discs with
d-pc and rear disc

Tyres: Front is 110/90V–16
Rear is 130/80V–18

Dimensions:
Length: 2145 mm
Width: 740 mm
Wheelbase: 1465 mm
Clearance: 145 mm
Seat height: 795 mm
Dry weight: 218 kg
Fuel tank: 22 litres

Performance:
Top speed: 220 km/h
Fuel consumption: 6.6 l/100 km

Features: One-way clutch
mechanism for smooth down
shifts. Hydraulic valve adjusters.

Manufacturer: Honda Motor Co. Ltd.

HONDA (Japan)

Model: VF750F-D/E

Engine: 4-str LC dohc
16-valve vee 4
Capacity: 748 cc
Bore × Stroke: 70 × 48.6 mm
Compression ratio: 10.5:1
Carburettor: 4/30 mm cv Keihin
Maximum power: 90 bhp
(DIN) at 10 000 rpm
Starting: electric

Transmission: 5-speed with
chain drive

Electrics: Transistorised 12 v
with electronic advance

Frame: Box section cradle

Suspension: Air-assisted front
fork with rear 4-way adjustable
Pro-Link system

Brakes: Twin front discs with
d-pc and rear disc

Tyres: Front is 120/80V–16
Rear is 130/80V–18

Dimensions:
Length: 2 210 mm
Width: 770 mm
Wheelbase: 1 495 mm
Clearance: 155 mm
Seat height: 820 mm
Dry weight: 218 kg
Fuel tank: 22 litres

Performance:
Top speed: 215 km/h
Fuel consumption: 7 l/100 km

Features: One-way clutch
mechanism. Frame-mounted
fairing.

Manufacturer: Honda Motor Co. Ltd.

HONDA (Japan)

Model: GL650D2 Silver Wing

Engine: 4-str LC ohv 8-valve
vee-twin
Capacity: 673 cc
Bore × Stroke: 82.5 × 63 mm
Compression ratio: 9.8:1
Carburettor: 2/39 mm cv Keihin
Maximum power: 64 bhp
(DIN) at 8 000 rpm
Starting: electric

Transmission: 5-speed with
shaft drive

Electrics: Transistorised 12 v
ignition with 14 Ah battery

Frame: Tubular spine

Suspension: Air-assisted fork
with rear air-assisted *Pro-Link*
system

Manufacturer: Honda Motor Co. Ltd.

Brakes: Twin front discs with
d-pc and rear drum

Tyres: Front is 120/80–18
Rear is 120/80–18

Dimensions:
Length: 2 305 mm
Width: 885 mm
Wheelbase: 1 495 mm
Clearance: 145 mm
Seat height: 770 mm
Dry weight: 240 kg
Fuel tank: 17.6 litres

Performance:
Top speed: 170 km/h
Fuel consumption: 6 l/100 km

Features: Lockable panniers
and many low maintenance
features.

HONDA (Japan)

Model: CX650E-D

Engine: 4-str LC ohv 8-valve
vee-twin
Capacity: 674 cc
Bore × Stroke: 82.5 × 63 mm
Compression ratio: 9.8:1
Carburettor: 2/35 mm Keihin
Maximum power: 64 bhp
(DIN) at 8 000 rpm
Starting: electric

Transmission: 5-speed with
shaft drive

Electrics: Transistorised 12 v
with electronic advance

Frame: Tubular spine

Suspension: Air-assisted front
fork with *TRAC* and rear
Pro-Link system

Brakes: Twin front discs with
d-pc and rear disc

Tyres: Front is 100/90–18 56H
Rear is 120/80–18 62H

Dimensions:
Length: 2 250 mm
Width: 760 mm
Wheelbase: 1 500 mm
Clearance: 150 mm
Seat height: 790 mm
Dry weight: 210 kg
Fuel tank: 19 litres

Performance:
Top speed: 185 km/h
Fuel consumption: 6.4 l/100 km

Features: Handlebar mounted
fairing.

Manufacturer: Honda Motor Co. Ltd.

HONDA (Japan)

Model: XL600LM-F

Engine: 4-str sohc RFVC
single
Capacity: 591 cc
Bore × Stroke: 97 × 80 mm
Compression ratio: 9:1
Carburettor: 2/28 mm Keihin
Maximum power: 44 bhp
(DIN) at 6000 rpm
Starting: electric

Transmission: 5-speed with
chain drive

Electrics: 12 v CDI ignition

Frame: Box section cradle

Suspension: Air-assisted
leading axle fork with rear
adjustable *Pro-Link* system

Brakes: Front disc with d-pc
and rear drum

Tyres: Front is 3.00–21
Rear is 5.10–17 (Tubeless)

Dimensions:
Length: 2135 mm
Width: 830 mm
Wheelbase: 1446 mm
Clearance: 265 mm
Seat height: 890 m
Dry weight: 149 kg
Fuel tank: 28 litres

Performance:
Top speed: 107 km/h
Fuel consumption: ...

Features: Paris–Dakar rally
styling. Dry sump lubrication
system. RFVC is Radial Four
Valve Combustion system.

Manufacturer: Honda Motor Co. Ltd.

HONDA (Japan)

Model: VF500F2-F

Engine: 4-str LC dohc
16-valve vee 4
Capacity: 498 cc
Bore × Stroke: 60 × 44 mm
Compression ratio: 11:1
Carburettor: 4/32 mm cv Keihin
Maximum power: 70 bhp
(DIN) at 10 500 rpm
Starting: electric

Transmission: 6-speed with
chain drive

Electrics: Transistorised 12 v
with electronic advance

Frame: Box section

Suspension: Air-assisted front
fork with *TRAC* and 4-way
adjustable *Pro-Link*

Brakes: Twin front discs with
d-pc and rear disc

Tyres: Front is 100/90V-16
Rear is 110/90V-18

Dimensions:
Length: 2 070 mm
Width: 760 mm
Wheelbase: 1 420 mm
Clearance: 135 mm
Seat height: 800 mm
Dry weight: 184 kg
Fuel tank: 16.5 litres

Performance:
Top speed: 205 km/h
Fuel consumption: 6.4 l/100 km

Features: Removable
downtube in frame for easier
engine maintenance.

Manufacturer: Honda Motor Co. Ltd.

HONDA (Japan)

Model: VT500E-D

Engine: 4-str LC sohc 6-valve
vee-twin
Capacity: 490 cc
Bore × Stroke: 71 × 62 mm
Compression ratio: 10.5:1
Carburettor: 2/32 mm cv Keihin
Maximum power: 52 bhp
(DIN) at 9 000 rpm
Starting: electric

Transmission: 6-speed with
enclosed shaft drive

Electrics: Transistorised 12 v
with electronic control

Frame: Duplex tubular cradle

Suspension: Air-assisted front
fork with twin rear hydraulic
shocks

Brakes: In-board ventilated
front disc and rear drum

Tyres: Front is 100/90–18 56S
Rear is 120/80–18 62S

Dimensions:
Length: 2 195 mm
Width: 760 mm
Wheelbase: 1 480 mm
Clearance: 165 mm
Seat height: 790 mm
Dry weight: 177 kg
Fuel tank: 18 litres

Performance:
Top speed: 180 km/h
Fuel consumption: 6 l/100 km

Features: Electric fan-
equipped radiator. Handlebar
mounted fairing.

Manufacturer: Honda Motor Co. Ltd.

HONDA (Japan)

Model: XBR500-F

Engine: 4-str sohc 4-valve
RFVC single
Capacity: 499 cc
Bore × Stroke: 92 × 75 mm
Compression ratio: 9.2:1
Carburettor: 39 mm Keihin
Maximum power: 44 bhp
(DIN) at 7000 rpm
Starting: electric/kick

Transmission: 5-speed with
chain drive

Electrics: 12 v CDI ignition

Frame: Semi-double cradle

Suspension: Telescopic front
fork with twin rear adjustable
shocks

Manufacturer: Honda Motor Co. Ltd.

Brakes: 276 mm front disc
and rear drum

Tyres: Front is 100/90–18
Rear is 110/90–18

Dimensions:
Length: 2100 mm
Width: 695 mm
Wheelbase: 1400 mm
Clearance: 165 mm
Seat height: 780 mm
Dry weight: 150 kg
Fuel tank: 20 litres

Performance:
Top speed: 165 km/h
Fuel consumption: 5 l/100 km

Features: Big single with
radial Four Valve Combustion
system.

HONDA (Japan)

Model: NS400R-F

Engine: 2-str LC vee three
with ATAC
Capacity: 387 cc
Bore × Stroke: 57 × 50.6 mm
Compression ratio: 6.7:1
Carburettor: 3/26 mm Keihin
Maximum power: 72 bhp
(DIN) at 9 500 rpm
Starting: kick

Transmission: 6-speed with
chain drive

Electrics: 12 v CDI ignition

Frame: Aluminium box section

Suspension: Air-assisted fork
with *TRAC* and rear remotely
controlled *Pro-Link*

Brakes: Triple-disc system
with d-pc

Tyres: Front is 100/90V-16
Rear is 110/90V-17

Dimensions:
Length: 2 063 mm
Width: 720 mm
Wheelbase: 1 394 mm
Clearance: 135 mm
Seat height: 792 mm
Dry weight: 164 kg
Fuel tank: 19 litres

Performance:
Top speed: 200 km/h
Fuel consumption: 9 l/100 km

Features: Automatic Torque
Amplification Chamber to
improve power at all rpm.
TRAC.

Manufacturer: Honda Motor Co. Ltd.

HONDA (Japan)

Model: VF400F-D

Engine: 4-str LC dohc
16-valve vee four
Capacity: 399 cc
Bore × Stroke: 55 × 42 mm
Compression ratio: 11:1
Carburettor: 4/30 mm cv Keihin
Maximum power: 55 bhp
(DIN) at 10 500 rpm
Starting: electric

Transmission: 6-speed with
chain drive

Electrics: Transistorised 12 v
with electronic advance

Frame: Duplex tubular cradle

Suspension: Air-assisted forks
with *TRAC* and rear air-assisted
Pro-Link

Brakes: In-board ventilated
disc at front and rear

Tyres: Front is 100/90–16 54H
Rear is 110/90–18 61H

Dimensions:
Length: 2 085 mm
Width: 750 mm
Wheelbase: 1 415 mm
Clearance: 140 mm
Seat height: 780 mm
Dry weight: 175 kg
Fuel tank: 17 litres

Performance:
Top speed: 180 km/h
Fuel consumption: 5.5 l/100 km

Features: Torque Reaction
Anti-dive Control. Tubeless
tyres.

Manufacturer: Honda Motor Co. Ltd.

HONDA (Japan)

Model: VT250F-D

Engine: 4-str LC dohc 8-valve
vee-twin
Capacity: 248 cc
Bore × Stroke: 60 × 44 mm
Compression ratio: 11:1
Carburettor: 2/32 mm cv Keihin
Maximum power: 35 bhp
(DIN) at 10 500 rpm
Starting: electric

Transmission: 6-speed with
chain drive

Electrics: Transistorised 12 v
with electronic advance

Frame: Duplex tubular cradle

Suspension: Air-assisted front
fork with rear air-assisted
Pro-Link

Brakes: Front ventilated disc
and rear drum

Tyres: Front is 100/90–16 54S
Rear is 110/80–18 58S

Dimensions:
Length: 2 027 mm
Width: 750 mm
Wheelbase: 1 385 mm
Clearance: 160 mm
Seat height: 780 mm
Dry weight: 149 kg
Fuel tank: 12 litres

Performance:
Top speed: 160 km/h
Fuel consumption: 5 l/100 km

Features: First 16″ front
wheel on a production 250.
Uses novel planetary gear
change mechanism.

Manufacturer: Honda Motor Co. Ltd.

HONDA (Japan)

Model: CBX250RS-E

Engine: 4-str RFVC dohc single
Capacity: 249 cc
Bore × Stroke: 72 × 61.3 mm
Compression ratio: 10.5:1
Carburettor: 2/26 mm Keihin
Maximum power: 31 bhp (DIN) at 9 500 rpm
Starting: electric

Transmission: 6-speed with chain drive

Electrics: 12 v CDI ignition with electronic advance

Frame: Tubular single cradle

Suspension: Telescopic front fork with twin rear hydraulic shocks

Brakes: Front disc with d-pc and rear drum

Tyres: Front is 90/90–18 51S
Rear is 110/90–18 61S

Dimensions:
Length: 2 020 mm
Width: 745 mm
Wheelbase: 1 360 mm
Clearance: 175 mm
Seat height: 770 mm
Dry weight: 129 kg
Fuel tank: 15 litres

Performance:
Top speed: 165 km/h
Fuel consumption: 5 l/100 km

Features: Radial Four Valve Combustion system. CB125RS-D is a 12 bhp, 124 cc model.

Manufacturer: Honda Motor Co. Ltd.

HONDA (Japan)

Model: CH250-F Spacy

Engine: 4-str LC sohc single
Capacity: 244 cc
Bore × Stroke: 72 × 60 mm
Compression ratio: 9.8:1
Carburettor: 30 mm cv Keihin
Maximum power: 21 bhp
(DIN) at 5 500 rpm
Starting: electric

Transmission: Honda
V-Matic with automatic clutch

Electrics: 12v CDI ignition

Frame: Monocoque

Suspension: Leading link fork
with twin rear hydraulic shocks

Brakes: Front disc with d-pc
and rear drum

Tyres: 4.00–10 tubeless at
front and rear

Dimensions:
Length: 1 920 mm
Width: 710 mm
Wheelbase: 1 280 mm
Clearance: 130 mm
Seat height: 750 mm
Dry weight: 122 kg
Fuel tank: 8 litres

Performance:
Top speed: 110 km/h
Fuel consumption: 3.2 l/100 km

Features: Scooter range also
includes the 125 cc Spacy and
the NH80/125 cc Lead.

Manufacturer: Honda Motor Co. Ltd.

HONDA (Japan)

Model: MBX125F-E

Engine: 2-str LC single
Capacity: 124 cc
Bore × Stroke: 56 × 50.6 mm
Compression ratio: 7.5:1
Carburettor: 24 mm Keihin
Maximum power: 12 bhp
(DIN) at 7 500 rpm
Starting: kick

Transmission: 6-speed with
chain drive

Electrics: 12 v CDI ignition

Frame: Tubular single cradle

Suspension: Air-assisted front
fork with rear *Pro-Link* system

Brakes: Front disc with d-pc
and rear drum

Tyres: Front is 80/100-16 45P
Rear is 90/90-18 51P

Dimensions:
Length: 1 970 mm
Width: 700 mm
Wheelbase: 1 310 mm
Clearance: 160 mm
Seat height: 760 mm
Dry weight: 99 kg
Fuel tank: 13 litres

Performance:
Top speed: 118 km/h
Fuel consumption: 4.2 l/100 km

Features: Series also includes
the 79 cc MBX80FWD and the
MBX50s sports moped.

Manufacturer: Honda Motor Co. Ltd.

HONDA (Japan)

Model: MTX125RW-F

Engine: 2-str LC reed valve single
Capacity: 124 cc
Bore × Stroke: 56 × 50.6 mm
Compression ratio: 7.5:1
Carburettor: 24 mm Keihin
Maximum power: 12 bhp (DIN) at 7 500 rpm
Starting: kick

Transmission: 6-speed with chain drive

Electrics: 12 v CDI ignition with 3 Ah battery

Frame: Tubular cradle

Suspension: Air-assisted leading axle fork with rear *Pro-Link* system

Brakes: Front disc with d-pc and rear drum

Tyres: Front is 2.75–21 4PR
Rear is 4.10–18 4PR

Dimensions:
Length: 2 090 mm
Width: 830 mm
Wheelbase: 1 345 mm
Clearance: 285 mm
Seat height: 845 mm
Dry weight: 99 kg
Fuel tank: 9 litres

Performance:
Top speed: 90 km/h
Fuel consumption: 4.2 l/100 km

Features: This motocross styled series includes the 9 bhp MTX80R, the 25 bhp MTX200R and the MT50S sports moped.

Manufacturer: Honda Motor Co. Ltd.

HONDA (Japan)

Model: CB125T Super Dream

Engine: 4-str sohc twin
Capacity: 124 cc
Bore × Stroke: 44 × 41 mm
Compression ratio: 9.4:1
Carburettor: 2/22 mm Keihin
Maximum power: 12 bhp
(DIN) at 9 000 rpm
Starting: electric

Transmission: 5-speed with
chain drive

Electrics: 12 v CDI ignition

Frame: Tubular single cradle

Suspension: Telescopic front
fork with rear *Pro-Link* system

Brakes: Front disc with d-pc
and rear drum

Tyres: Front is 3.00–18 4PR
Rear is 3.25–18 4PR

Dimensions:
Length: 2 060 mm
Width: 720 mm
Wheelbase: 1 350 mm
Clearance: 165 mm
Seat height: 770 mm
Dry weight: 125 kg
Fuel tank: 13 litres

Performance:
Top speed: 118 km/h
Fuel consumption: 2 l/100 km

Features: CB series includes
125RS single and the 100N
with a 99 cc 4-str single
engine.

Manufacturer: Honda Motor Co. Ltd.

HONDA (Japan)

Model: CM125C-F

Engine: 4-str sohc parallel twin
Capacity: 124 cc
Bore × Stroke: 44 × 41 mm
Compression ratio: 9.4:1
Carburettor: 22 mm Keihin
Maximum power: 12 bhp (DIN) at 9 500 rpm
Starting: electric

Transmission: 5-speed with chain drive

Electrics: Transistorised 12 v with electronic advance

Frame: Tubular single cradle

Suspension: Telescopic front fork with twin rear hydraulic shocks

Manufacturer: Honda Motor Co. Ltd.

Brakes: Drums at front and rear

Tyres: Front is 3.25–18 4PR
Rear is 110/90–16 4PR

Dimensions:
Length: 2 065 mm
Width: 810 mm
Wheelbase: 1 350 mm
Clearance: 165 mm
Seat height: 750 mm
Dry weight: 128 kg
Fuel tank: 12.5 litres

Performance:
Top speed: 113 km/h
Fuel consumption: 3 l/100 km

Features: King and Queen style seat.

HONDA (Japan)

Model: XL125R-F

Engine: 4-str sohc single
Capacity: 124 cc
Bore × Stroke: 56.5 × 49.5 mm
Compression ratio: 9.4:1
Carburettor: 22 mm Keihin
Maximum power: 12 bhp
(DIN) at 9 000 rpm
Starting: kick

Transmission: 6-speed with
chain drive

Electrics: 12 v CDI ignition

Frame: Tubular diamond

Suspension: Air-assisted
leading axle fork with 5-way
adjustable *Pro-Link*

Manufacturer: Honda Motor Co. Ltd.

Brakes: Front disc with d-pc
and rear drum

Tyres: Front is 2.75–21 4PR
Rear is 4.10–18 4PR

Dimensions:
Length: 2 080 mm
Width: 840 mm
Wheelbase: 1 355 mm
Clearance: 270 mm
Seat height: 840 mm
Dry weight: 107 kg
Fuel tank: 7 litres

Performance:
Top speed: 160 km/h
Fuel consumption: ...

Features: XL series includes
250R (25 bhp) and the 600R
(44 bhp).

HONDA (Japan)

Model: CG125-F

Engine: 4-str sohc single
Capacity: 124 cc
Bore × Stroke: 56.5 × 49.5 mm
Compression ratio: 9.2:1
Carburettor: 24 mm Keihin
Maximum power: 11 bhp
(DIN) at 9 000 rpm
Starting: kick

Transmission: 5-speed with
chain drive

Electrics: 12 v coil ignition
and battery

Frame: Tubular single cradle

Suspension: Telescopic front
fork with twin rear hydraulic
dampers

Brakes: Drums at front and
rear

Tyres: Front is 2.50–18 4PR
Rear is 3.00–17 6PR

Dimensions:
Length: 1 935 mm
Width: 745 mm
Wheelbase: 1 280 mm
Clearance: 150 mm
Seat height: 755 mm
Dry weight: 99 kg
Fuel tank: 12 litres

Performance:
Top speed: 105 km/h
Fuel consumption: 2 l/100 km

Features: Power Fuel Control
System for increased fuel
economy.

Manufacturer: Honda Motor Co. Ltd.

HONDA (Japan)

Model: C90M-F Cub

Engine: 4-str sohc single
Capacity: 85 cc
Bore × Stroke: 47 × 49.5 mm
Compression ratio: 8.8:1
Carburettor: 16 mm Keihin
Maximum power: 7.5 bhp
(DIN) at 5 500 rpm
Starting: electric

Transmission: 3-speed
automatic with chain drive

Electrics: 12 v CDI ignition
with 5 Ah battery

Frame: Step-thru

Suspension: Leading link
front fork with twin rear
dampers

Brakes: 120 mm drums front
and rear

Tyres: Front is 2.50–17 4PR
Rear is 2.50–17 6PR

Dimensions:
Length: 1 835 mm
Width: 660 mm
Wheelbase: 1 175 mm
Clearance: 130 mm
Seat height: 750 mm
Dry weight: 82 kg
Fuel tank: 4 litres

Performance:
Top speed: 80 km/h
Fuel consumption: 2 l/100 km

Features: Cub range includes
the C50 and C70 versions.

Manufacturer: Honda Motor Co. Ltd.

HONDA (Japan)

Model: NV50MS-D Stream

Engine: 2-str piston port
single
Capacity: 49 cc
Bore × Stroke: 40 × 39.3 mm
Compression ratio: 6.8:1
Carburettor: 12 mm Keihin
Maximum power: 3.26 bhp
(DIN) at 6 000 rpm
Starting: electric

Transmission: Honda
V-Matic with automatic clutch

Electrics: 12 v CDI ignition

Frame: Monocoque

Suspension: Leading link fork
with rear swinging link
assembly

Brakes: Drums at front and
rear

Tyres: 3.00–8 2PR at front
and rear

Dimensions:
Length: 1 665 mm
Width: 570 mm
Wheelbase: 1 210 mm
Clearance: 95 mm
Seat height: 665 mm
Dry weight: 76 kg
Fuel tank: 4 litres

Performance:
Top speed: 57 km/h
Fuel consumption: 2.4 l/100 km

Features: 3-wheel moped
with a swivelling mechanism to
let the main body lean on
cornering.

Manufacturer: Honda Motor Co. Ltd.

HONDA (Japan)

Model: PXR50

Engine: 2-str piston port
single
Capacity: 49 cc
Bore × Stroke: 40 × 39.3 mm
Compression ratio: 6.5:1
Carburettor: 12 mm Keihin
Maximum power: 2.46 bhp
(DIN) at 3 500 rpm
Starting: electric

Transmission: Honda
V-Matic with automatic clutch

Electrics: 12 v CDI ignition

Frame: Tubular spine

Suspension: Telescopic front
fork with rear single damper

Manufacturer: Honda Motor Co. Ltd.

Brakes: Drums at front and
rear

Tyres: Front is 2.50–17
Rear is 2.75–14

Dimensions:
Length: 1 750 mm
Width: 680 mm
Wheelbase: 1 130 mm
Clearance: 150 mm
Seat height: 815 mm
Dry weight: 61 kg
Fuel tank: 4 litres

Performance:
Top speed: 55 km/h
Fuel consumption: 2 l/100 km

Features: Sports style moped.

HONDA (Japan)

Model: PA50 Camino

Engine: 2-str piston port single
Capacity: 49 cc
Bore × Stroke: 40 × 39.6 mm
Compression ratio: 6.7:1
Carburettor: 12 mm, Keihin
Maximum power: 2.3 bhp (DIN) at 5 500 rpm
Starting: pedal

Transmission: Honda V-Matic with automatic clutch

Electrics: Flywheel magneto 6 v ignition

Frame: Pressed steel spine

Suspension: Telescopic front fork with twin rear dampers

Manufacturer: Honda Motor Co. Ltd.

Brakes: Drums at front and rear

Tyres: 2.00–17 at front and rear

Dimensions:
Length: 1 650 mm
Width: 620 mm
Wheelbase: 1 055 mm
Clearance: 120 mm
Seat height: 775 mm
Dry weight: 47 kg
Fuel tank: 3 litres

Performance:
Top speed: 45 km/h
Fuel consumption: 2 l/100 km

Features: Adjustable seat and fully enclosed drive chain.

HOREX (West Germany)

Model: HRD600

Engine: 4-str Rotax sohc 4-valve single
Capacity: 562 cc
Bore × Stroke: 94 × 81 mm
Compression ratio: 9.6:1
Carburettor: 40 mm Bing
Maximum power: 50 bhp
Starting: electric/kick

Transmission: 5-speed with chain drive

Electrics: Transistorised 12 v ignition

Frame: Chrome-moly tubular

Suspension: Air-assisted front fork with adjustable rear monoshock system

Brakes: Twin 280 mm Brembo discs and 260 mm rear disc

Tyres: Front is 110/90–16 Rear is 130/90–16

Dimensions:
Length: ...
Width: ...
Wheelbase: 1 430 mm
Clearance: ...
Seat height: ...
Dry weight: 140 kg
Fuel tank: 17 litres

Performance:
Top speed: ...
Fuel consumption: ...

Features: Type 500 has 27 bhp 494 cc engine.

Manufacturer: Zweirad Röth GmbH & Co, Schulstrasse 6, 6149 Hammelbach, Odenwald, West Germany.

HOREX (West Germany)

Model: HRD80SS

Engine: 2-str Fichtel & Sachs
single
Capacity: 79.8 cc
Bore × Stroke: 46 × 48 mm
Compression ratio: 10:1
Carburettor: 20 mm Bing
Maximum power: 9 bhp
(DIN) at 6 000 rpm
Starting: kick

Transmission: 5-speed with
chain drive

Electrics: Transistorised 12 v
ignition with 9 Ah battery

Frame: Chrome-moly tubular

Suspension: Telescopic front
fork with rear adjustable
monoshock system

Manufacturer: Zweirad Röth GmbH & Co.

Brakes: 260 mm Brembo disc
and 160 mm rear drum

Tyres: Front is 3.00–18
Rear is 3.50–18

Dimensions:
Length: 2 000 mm
Width: 620 mm
Wheelbase: 1 340 mm
Clearance: ...
Seat height: ...
Dry weight: 104 kg
Fuel tank: 9.5 litres

Performance:
Top speed: ...
Fuel consumption: ...

Features: ...

HRD (Italy)

Model: Silver Horse 125

Engine: 2-str LC rotary valve
single
Capacity: 124.6 cc
Bore × Stroke: 56 × 50.6 mm
Compression ratio: 16:1
Carburettor: 28 mm Dell'Orto
Maximum power: 28 bhp
Starting: kick

Transmission: 6-speed with
chain drive

Electrics: Transistorised 12 v
Motoplat ignition

Frame: Chrome-moly cradle

Suspension: Telescopic front
fork with rear monoshock
system

Brakes: 240 mm triple disc
system

Tyres: Front is 100/90–16
Rear is 130/90–16

Dimensions:
Length: 2 000 mm
Width: 620 mm
Wheelbase: 1 350 mm
Clearance: ...
Seat height: 820 mm
Dry weight: 106 kg
Fuel tank: ...

Performance:
Top speed: over 145 km/h
Fuel consumption: ...

Features: ...

Manufacturer: HRD Motor S.p.A., via G. Puccini 15,
20028 S. Vittore Olona (MI), Italy.

HRD (Italy)

Model: Red Horse 125

Engine: 2-str LC rotary valve
single
Capacity: 124.6 cc
Bore × Stroke: 56 × 50.6 mm
Compression ratio: 14.5:1
Carburettor: 28 mm Dell'Orto
Maximum power: 26 bhp
(DIN) at 9 750 rpm
Starting: kick

Transmission: 6-speed with
chain drive

Electrics: Transistorised 12 v
Motoplat ignition

Frame: Chrome-moly cradle

Suspension: Telescopic front
fork with rear monoshock
system

Manufacturer: HRD Motor S.p.A.

Brakes: 260 mm front disc
and 160 mm rear drum

Tyres: Front is 3.00–18
Rear is 120/90–16

Dimensions:
Length: 2 000 mm
Width: 620 mm
Wheelbase: 1 350 mm
Clearance: ...
Seat height: 820 mm
Dry weight: 104 kg
Fuel tank: ...

Performance:
Top speed: 140 km/h
Fuel consumption: 6 l/100 km

Features: ...

HRD (Italy)

Model: WH125 Road

Engine: 2-str LC rotary valve single
Capacity: 124.6 cc
Bore × Stroke: 56 × 50.6 mm
Compression ratio: 16:1
Carburettor: 28 mm Dell'Orto
Maximum power: 24 bhp
Starting: electric

Transmission: 6-speed with chain drive

Electrics: Transistorised 12 v Motoplat ignition

Frame: Chrome-moly cradle

Suspension: Telescopic front fork with rear monoshock system

Manufacturer: HRD Motor S.p.A.

Brakes: 260 mm front disc and 160 mm rear drum

Tyres: Front is 3.00–18
Rear is 120/90–16

Dimensions:
Length: 2 000 mm
Width: 680 mm
Wheelbase: 1 350 mm
Clearance: ...
Seat height: 810 mm
Dry weight: 105 kg
Fuel tank: ...

Performance:
Top speed: 135 km/h
Fuel consumption: ...

Features: ...

HUSQVARNA (Sweden)

Model: 510

Engine: 4-str sohc 4-valve single
Capacity: 503 cc
Bore × Stroke: 91.5 × 76.5 mm
Compression ratio: 9.5:1
Carburettor: 40 mm Dell'Orto
Maximum power: ...
Starting: kick

Transmission: 6-speed with chain drive

Electrics: SEM CDI 12 v ignition

Frame: Chrome-moly cradle

Suspension: Leading axle fork with rear adjustable *Öhlins* monoshock system

Brakes: 230 mm front disc and 160 mm rear drum

Tyres: Front is 3.00–21
Rear is 4.50–18

Dimensions:
Length: 2 220 mm
Width: ...
Wheelbase: 1 480 mm
Clearance: 345 mm
Seat height: 940 mm
Dry weight: 117 kg
Fuel tank: 9 litres

Performance:
Top speed: ...
Fuel consumption: ...

Features: Aluminium swinging arm.

Manufacturer: Husqvarna Motorcyklar AB, Box 103 S, 59900 Ödeshög, Sweden.

HUSQVARNA (Sweden)

Model: 430

Engine: 2-str LC single
Capacity: 430 cc
Bore × Stroke: 86 × 74 mm
Compression ratio: 12.6:1
Carburettor: 38 mm Mikuni
Maximum power: ...
Starting: kick

Transmission: Automatic with
chain drive

Electrics: SEM CDI 12 v
ignition

Frame: Chrome-moly cradle

Suspension: Leading axle fork
with rear adjustable *Öhlins*
monoshock system

Brakes: 260 mm front disc
and 160 mm rear drum

Tyres: Front is 3.00–21
Rear is 5.00–18

Dimensions:
Length: ...
Width: ...
Wheelbase: 1 504 mm
Clearance: 345 mm
Seat height: 940 mm
Dry weight: 107 kg
Fuel tank: 12 litres

Performance:
Top speed: ...
Fuel consumption: ...

Features: ...

Manufacturer: Husqvarna Motorcyklar AB.

HUSQVARNA (Sweden)

Model: MC250MP

Engine: 2-str piston port single
Capacity: 250 cc
Bore × Stroke: 69.5 × 64.5 mm
Compression ratio: 11.8:1
Carburettor: 38 mm Mikuni
Maximum power: 20 bhp
Starting: kick

Transmission: 4-speed with automatic drive

Electrics: SEM CDI 12 v ignition

Frame: Tubular cradle

Suspension: Telescopic front fork with twin rear shock absorbers

Brakes: Drums with the rear brake operable by foot or lever

Tyres: Front is 3.50–21
Rear is 4.50–17

Dimensions:
Length: 2 220 mm
Width: 860 mm
Wheelbase: 1 480 mm
Clearance: 280 mm
Seat height: 900 mm
Dry weight: 130 kg
Fuel tank: ...

Performance:
Top speed: 110 km/h
Fuel consumption: ...

Features: Multi-purpose bike used by Swedish Armed Forces. Can be fitted with skis.

Manufacturer: Husqvarna Motorcyklar AB.

HUSQVARNA (Sweden)

Model: 125WR

Engine: 2-str LC single
Capacity: 124 cc
Bore × Stroke: 55 × 52 mm
Compression ratio: 15.8:1
Carburettor: 36 mm Mikuni
Maximum power: ...
Starting: kick

Transmission: 6-speed with chain drive

Electrics: SEM CDI 12 v ignition

Frame: Chrome-moly cradle

Suspension: Leading axle fork with rear adjustable *Öhlins* monoshock system

Brakes: 160 mm drums at front and rear

Tyres: Front is 3.00–21
Rear is 4.50–18

Dimensions:
Length: 2 220 mm
Width: ...
Wheelbase: 1 480 mm
Clearance: 365 mm
Seat height: 960 mm
Dry weight: 97 kg
Fuel tank: 10 litres

Performance:
Top speed: ...
Fuel consumption: ...

Features: Series includes 250WR and 400WR Enduro bikes.

Manufacturer: Husqvarna Motorcyklar AB.

JAWA (Czechoslovakia)

Model: Jawa-Velorex

Engine: 2-str piston port twin
Capacity: 343.47 cc
Bore × Stroke: 58 × 65 mm
Compression ratio: 10.2:1
Carburettor: 28 mm Jikov
Maximum power: 26 bhp
(DIN) at 5 250 rpm
Starting: kick

Transmission: 4-speed with
chain drive

Electrics: 12 v coil ignition
with 5 Ah battery

Frame: Duplex tubular cradle

Suspension: Telescopic front
fork with 4-way adjustable rear
shocks

Brakes: 160 mm drums at
front and rear

Tyres: Front is 3.25–18
Rear is 3.50–18
Sidecar 16″

Dimensions:
Length: 2 080 mm
Width: 1 473 mm
Wheelbase: 1 350 mm
Clearance: 130 mm
Seat height: 810 mm
Dry weight: 227 kg
Fuel tank: 17 litres

Performance:
Top speed: 114 km/h
Fuel consumption: 4.8 l/100 km

Features: Other sidecar
versions are Shadow Sport and
Tradesman.

Manufacturer: Jawa Týnec nad Sázavou, Czechoslovakia.

KAWASAKI (Japan)

Model: ZG1300-A1

Engine: 4-str LC dohc in-line six
Capacity: 1 286 cc
Bore × Stroke: 62 × 71 mm
Compression ratio: 9.9:1
Carburettor: fuel injection
Maximum power: 130 bhp (DIN) at 8 000 rpm
Starting: electric

Transmission: 5-speed with shaft drive

Electrics: Transistorised 12 v ignition with 20 Ah battery

Frame: Duplex tubular cradle

Suspension: Air-assisted front fork and rear 4-way adjustable air shocks

Brakes: Twin 260 mm front discs and 249 mm rear disc

Tyres: Front is 110/90V–18
Rear is 130/90V–17

Dimensions:
Length: 2 335 mm
Width: 855 mm
Wheelbase: 1 580 mm
Clearance: 145 mm
Seat height: 835 mm
Dry weight: 294 kg
Fuel tank: 27 litres

Performance:
Top speed: 235 km/h
Fuel consumption: 8 l/100 km

Features: Tubeless tyres. Digital fuel injection, sintered metal brake pads.

Manufacturer: Kawasaki Heavy Industries Ltd., 1–1 Kawasaki-cho, Akashi-city 673, Hyogo, Japan.

KAWASAKI (Japan)

Model: GPz1100

Engine: 4-str dohc in-line four
Capacity: 1 089 cc
Bore × Stroke: 72.5 × 66 mm
Compression ratio: 8.9:1
Carburettor: fuel injection
Maximum power: 120 bhp
(DIN) at 8 750 rpm
Starting: electric

Transmission: 5-speed with
chain drive

Electrics: Transistorised 12 v
ignition with 18 Ah battery

Frame: Duplex tubular cradle

Suspension: Air-assisted fork
with anti-dive and rear 4-way
adjustable *Uni-Trak*

Brakes: Twin 246 mm front
discs and 236 mm rear disc

Tyres: Front is 110/90V–18
Rear is 130/90V–17

Dimensions:
Length: 2 320 mm
Width: 740 mm
Wheelbase: 1 565 mm
Clearance: 140 mm
Seat height: 800 mm
Dry weight: 244 kg
Fuel tank: 20.4 litres

Performance:
Top speed: 240 km/h
Fuel consumption: 6 l/100 km

Features: Frame-mounted
fairing, tubeless tyres, 4-tier oil
cooler, positive neutral finder.

Manufacturer: Kawasaki Heavy Industries Ltd.

KAWASAKI (Japan)

Model: Z1100RI

Engine: 4-str dohc in-line four
Capacity: 1 089 cc
Bore × Stroke: 72.5 × 66 mm
Compression ratio: 9.5:1
Carburettor: 4/34 mm Mikuni
Maximum power: 114 bhp
(DIN) at 8 500 rpm
Starting: electric

Transmission: 5-speed with
chain drive

Electrics: Transistorised 12 v
ignition with 18 Ah battery

Frame: Duplex tubular cradle

Suspension: Air-assisted front
fork with adjustable piggy back
Kayaba rear shocks

Brakes: Twin 246 mm front
discs and 236 mm rear disc

Tyres: Front is 110/90V–18
Rear is 130/80V–18

Dimensions:
Length: 2 265 mm
Width: 785 mm
Wheelbase: 1 540 mm
Clearance: 140 mm
Seat height: 785 mm
Dry weight: 238 kg
Fuel tank: 21.4 litres

Performance:
Top speed: 232 km/h
Fuel consumption: 7 l/100 km

Features: Tubeless tyres,
4-tier oil cooler, positive neutral
finder.

Manufacturer: Kawasaki Heavy Industries Ltd.

KAWASAKI (Japan)

Model: Z1100-A3

Engine: 4-str dohc in-line four
Capacity: 1 089 cc
Bore x Stroke: 72.5 × 66 mm
Compression ratio: 8.9:1
Carburettor: 4/34 mm Mikuni
Maximum power: 100 bhp
(DIN) at 8 000 rpm
Starting: electric

Transmission: 5-speed with
shaft drive

Electrics: Transistorised 12 v
ignition with 18 Ah battery

Frame: Duplex tubular cradle

Suspension: Air-assisted
leading axle fork and rear
4-way air-adjustable shocks

Brakes: 236 mm triple disc
system

Tyres: Front is 3.50V–19
Rear is 130/90V–16

Dimensions:
Length: 2 310 mm
Width: 890 mm
Wheelbase: 1 545 mm
Clearance: 125 mm
Seat height: 790 mm
Dry weight: 246 kg
Fuel tank: 21.4 litres

Performance:
Top speed: 220 km/h
Fuel consumption: 7 l/100 km

Features: ...

Manufacturer: Kawasaki Heavy Industries Ltd.

KAWASAKI (Japan)

Model: GPz900R

Engine: 4-str LC dohc
16-valve in-line four
Capacity: 908 cc
Bore × Stroke: 72.5 × 55 mm
Compression ratio: 11:1
Carburettor: 4/34 mm Keihin
Maximum power: 115 bhp
(DIN) at 9 500 rpm
Starting: electric

Transmission: 6-speed with
chain drive

Electrics: Transistorised 12 v
ignition with 14 Ah battery

Frame: Tubular steel diamond

Suspension: Telehydraulic
fork with *AVDS*, adjustable
anti-dive and rear adjustable
Uni-Trak system

Brakes: Twin 280 mm front
discs and 270 mm rear disc

Tyres: Front is 120/80V–16
Rear is 130/80V–18

Dimensions:
Length: 2 200 mm
Width: 750 mm
Wheelbase: 1 495 mm
Clearance: 140 mm
Seat height: 780 mm
Dry weight: 228 kg
Fuel tank: 22 litres

Performance:
Top speed: 252 km/h
Fuel consumption: 6 l/100 km

Features: Automatic Variable
Damping System on front fork.
Tubeless tyres.

Manufacturer: Kawasaki Heavy Industries Ltd.

KAWASAKI (Japan)

Model: ZX750-E2

Engine: 4-str turbo dohc
in-line four
Capacity: 738 cc
Bore × Stroke: 66 × 54 mm
Compression ratio: 7.8:1
Carburettor: fuel injection
Maximum power: 112 bhp
(DIN) at 9000 rpm
Starting: electric

Transmission: 5-speed with
chain drive

Electrics: Transistorised 12 v
ignition with 14 Ah battery

Frame: Duplex tubular cradle

Suspension: Telehydraulic
fork with anti-dive and rear air-
adjustable *Uni-Trak*

Brakes: Twin 280 mm front
discs and 270 mm rear disc

Tyres: Front is 110/90V–18
Rear is 130/80V–18

Dimensions:
Length: 2220 mm
Width: 740 mm
Wheelbase: 1490 mm
Clearance: ...
Seat height: 780 mm
Dry weight: 233 kg
Fuel tank: 17 litres

Performance:
Top speed: 240 km/h
Fuel consumption: 8 l/100 km

Features: Tubeless tyres.

Manufacturer: Kawasaki Heavy Industries Ltd.

KAWASAKI (Japan)

Model: GPz750R

Engine: 4-str LC dohc
16-valve four
Capacity: 748 cc
Bore × Stroke: 70 × 48.6 mm
Compression ratio: 10.5:1
Carburettor: 4/32 mm Keihin
Maximum power: 92 bhp
(DIN) at 10 000 rpm
Starting: electric

Transmission: 6-speed with
chain drive

Electrics: Transistorised 12 v
ignition with 14 Ah battery

Frame: Tubular steel diamond

Suspension: Telehydraulic
fork with *AVDS*, adjustable
anti-dive and rear air-adjustable
Uni-Trak system

Brakes: Twin 280 mm front
discs and 270 mm rear disc

Tyres: Front is 120/80V–16
Rear is 130/80V–18

Dimensions:
Length: 2 200 mm
Width: 750 mm
Wheelbase: 1 495 mm
Clearance: 140 mm
Seat height: 780 mm
Dry weight: 228 kg
Fuel tank: 22 litres

Performance:
Top speed: 230 km/h
Fuel consumption: 6.2 l/100 km

Features: Tubeless tyres.
Automatic Variable Damping
System. Lightweight CVK flat
carbs.

Manufacturer: Kawasaki Heavy Industries Ltd.

KAWASAKI (Japan)

Model: Z750

Engine: 4-str dohc in-line four
Capacity: 738 cc
Bore × Stroke: 66 × 54 mm
Compression ratio: 9.5:1
Carburettor: 4/34 mm Mikuni
Maximum power: 80 bhp
(DIN) at 9 500 rpm
Starting: electric

Transmission: 5-speed with
chain drive

Electrics: Transistorised 12 v
ignition with 12 Ah battery

Frame: Duplex tubular cradle

Suspension: Air-adjustable
fork with rear adjustable shocks

Brakes: 226 mm triple disc
system

Tyres: Front is 100/90–19 57H
Rear is 120/90–18 65H

Dimensions:
Length: 2 215 mm
Width: 770 mm
Wheelbase: 1 460 mm
Clearance: 140 mm
Seat height: 800 mm
Dry weight: 215 kg
Fuel tank: 21.7 litres

Performance:
Top speed: 204 km/h
Fuel consumption: 5.6 l/100 km

Features: ...

Manufacturer: Kawasaki Heavy Industries Ltd.

KAWASAKI (Japan)

Model: GT750

Engine: 4-str dohc in-line four
Capacity: 738 cc
Bore × Stroke: 66 × 54 mm
Compression ratio: 9.5:1
Carburettor: 4/34 mm Mikuni
Maximum power: 78 bhp
(DIN) at 9 500 rpm
Starting: electric

Transmission: 5-speed with shaft drive

Electrics: Transistorised 12 v ignition with 14 Ah battery

Frame: Duplex tubular cradle

Suspension: Air-assisted fork with 4-way air-adjustable rear shocks

Brakes: 226 mm triple disc system

Tyres: Front is 100/90–19 57H
Rear is 120/90–18 65H

Dimensions:
Length: 2 255 mm
Width: 760 mm
Wheelbase: 1 480 mm
Clearance: 150 mm
Seat height: 800 mm
Dry weight: 220 kg
Fuel tank: 24.3 litres

Performance:
Top speed: 205 km/h
Fuel consumption: 6.5 l/100 km

Features: Tubeless tyres, positive neutral finder.

Manufacturer: Kawasaki Heavy Industries Ltd.

KAWASAKI (Japan)

Model: GPz600R

Engine: 4-str LC dohc
16-valve four
Capacity: 592 cc
Bore × Stroke: 60 × 52.4 mm
Compression ratio: 11:1
Carburettor: 4/32 mm Keihin
Maximum power: 75 bhp
(DIN) at 10 500 rpm
Starting: electric

Transmission: 6-speed with
chain drive

Electrics: Transistorised 12 v
ignition with 12 Ah battery

Frame: Box section cradle

Suspension: Telehydraulic
fork with *AVDS*, adjustable
anti-dive and rear adjustable
Uni-Trak system

Brakes: Twin 270 mm front
discs and 250 mm rear disc

Tyres: Front is 110/90V-16
Rear is 130/90V-16

Dimensions:
Length: 2 140 mm
Width: 670 mm
Wheelbase: 1 430 mm
Clearance: 140 mm
Seat height: 770 mm
Dry weight: 195 kg
Fuel tank: 18 litres

Performance:
Top speed: 216 km/h
Fuel consumption: 5 l/100 km

Features: Tubeless tyres.

Manufacturer: Kawasaki Heavy Industries Ltd.

KAWASAKI (Japan)

Model: KLR600

Engine: 4-str LC dohc 4-valve single
Capacity: 564 cc
Bore × Stroke: 96 × 78 mm
Compression ratio: 9.5:1
Carburettor: 40 mm Keihin
Maximum power: 42 bhp (DIN) at 7 000 rpm
Starting: electric

Transmission: 5-speed with chain drive

Electrics: 12 v CDI ignition with 12 Ah battery

Frame: Tubular single cradle

Suspension: Air-assisted leading axle fork with adjustable rear *Uni-Trak*

Brakes: 250 mm front disc and 130 mm rear drum

Tyres: Front is 90/90–21 54S
Rear is 130/80–17 65S

Dimensions:
Length: 2 240 mm
Width: 875 mm
Wheelbase: 1 494 mm
Clearance: 285 mm
Seat height: 870 mm
Dry weight: 146 kg
Fuel tank: 11.5 litres

Performance:
Top speed: 165 km/h
Fuel consumption: 6 l/100 km

Features: Kawasaki Automatic Compression Release mechanism.

Manufacturer: Kawasaki Heavy Industries Ltd.

KAWASAKI (Japan)

Model: GPz550

Engine: 4-str dohc in-line four
Capacity: 553 cc
Bore × Stroke: 58 × 52.4 mm
Compression ratio: 10:1
Carburettor: 4/27 mm Tekei
Maximum power: 65 bhp
(DIN) at 10 500 rpm
Starting: electric

Transmission: 6-speed with
chain drive

Electrics: Transistorised 12 v
ignition with 12 Ah battery

Frame: Duplex tubular cradle

Suspension: Telehydraulic
fork with anti-dive and
adjustable rear *Uni-Trak*

Brakes: 228 mm triple disc
system

Tyres: Front is 100/90–18 56H
Rear is 120/80–18 62H

Dimensions:
Length: 2 205 mm
Width: 720 mm
Wheelbase: 1 445 mm
Clearance: 160 mm
Seat height: 780 mm
Dry weight: 191 kg
Fuel tank: 18 litres

Performance:
Top speed: 205 km/h
Fuel consumption: 6 l/100 km

Features: Tubeless tyres, five-
tier oil cooler. Frame-mounted
fairing.

Manufacturer: Kawasaki Heavy Industries Ltd.

KAWASAKI (Japan)

Model: GT550

Engine: 4-str dohc in-line four
Capacity: 553 cc
Bore × Stroke: 58 × 52.4 mm
Compression ratio: 9.5:1
Carburettor: 4/26 mm Tekei
Maximum power: 56 bhp
(DIN) at 7 500 rpm
Starting: electric

Transmission: 6-speed with
shaft drive

Electrics: Transistorised 12 v
ignition with 12 Ah battery

Frame: Duplex tubular cradle

Suspension: Air-adjustable
fork with 4-way adjustable rear
shocks

Brakes: 240 mm twin front
discs and 178 mm rear drum

Tyres: Front is 100/90–19 57H
Rear is 120/90–18 65H

Dimensions:
Length: 2 230 mm
Width: 755 mm
Wheelbase: 1 475 mm
Clearance: 154 mm
Seat height: 800 mm
Dry weight: 201 kg
Fuel tank: 21.5 litres

Performance:
Top speed: 185 km/h
Fuel consumption: 5.6 l/100 km

Features: Tubeless tyres.

Manufacturer: Kawasaki Heavy Industries Ltd.

KAWASAKI (Japan)

Model: Z550F

Engine: 4-str dohc in-line four
Capacity: 553 cc
Bore × Stroke: 58 × 52.4 mm
Compression ratio: 9.5:1
Carburettor: 4/26 mm Tekei
Maximum power: 56 bhp
(DIN) at 9 000 rpm
Starting: electric

Transmission: 6-speed with
chain drive

Electrics: Transistorised 12 v
ignition with 12 Ah battery

Frame: Duplex tubular cradle

Suspension: Air-adjustable
fork with adjustable rear *Uni-
Trak* system

Brakes: Twin 240 mm front
discs and 160 mm rear drum

Tyres: Front is 3.25H–19
Rear is 4.00H–18

Dimensions:
Length: ...
Width: 750 mm
Wheelbase: 1 448 mm
Clearance: 160 mm
Seat height: 780 mm
Dry weight: 184 kg
Fuel tank: 19 litres

Performance:
Top speed: 185 km/h
Fuel consumption: 5.6 l/100 km

Features: Tubeless tyres.

Manufacturer: Kawasaki Heavy Industries Ltd.

KAWASAKI (Japan)

Model: LTD450

Engine: 4-str LC dohc 8-valve twin
Capacity: 454 cc
Bore × Stroke: 72.5 × 55 mm
Compression ratio: 10.7:1
Carburettor: 2/34 mm Keihin
Maximum power: 50 bhp (DIN) at 9 500 rpm
Starting: electric

Transmission: 6-speed with Polychain belt drive

Electrics: Transistorised 12 v ignition with 12 Ah battery

Frame: Duplex tubular cradle

Suspension: Long leading axle fork with twin rear adjustable shocks

Brakes: 228 mm front disc and 160 mm rear drum

Tyres: Front is 100/90–19 57S
Rear is 140/90–15 70S

Dimensions:
Length: 2 210 mm
Width: 820 mm
Wheelbase: 1 485 mm
Clearance: 140 mm
Seat height: 745 mm
Dry weight: 181 kg
Fuel tank: 11 litres

Performance:
Top speed: 172 km/h
Fuel consumption: 5 l/100 km

Features: Custom styling, tubeless tyres.

Manufacturer: Kawasaki Heavy Industries Ltd.

KAWASAKI (Japan)

Model: Z400FII

Engine: 4-str dohc in-line four
Capacity: 399 cc
Bore × Stroke: 55 × 42 mm
Compression ratio: 9.7:1
Carburettor: 4/30 mm Keihin
Maximum power: 54 bhp
(DIN) at 11 500 rpm
Starting: electric

Transmission: 6-speed with
chain drive

Electrics: Transistorised 12 v
ignition with 10 Ah battery

Frame: Duplex tubular cradle

Suspension: Air-assisted fork
with anti-dive and adjustable
rear *Uni-Trak*

Brakes: Twin 240 mm front
discs and 160 mm rear drum

Tyres: Front is 100/90–18 56H
Rear is 110/90–18 61H

Dimensions:
Length: 2 180 mm
Width: 720 mm
Wheelbase: 1 435 mm
Clearance: 160 mm
Seat height: 780 mm
Dry weight: 179 kg
Fuel tank: 18 litres

Performance:
Top speed: 185 km/h
Fuel consumption: . . .

Features: Tubeless tyres.

Manufacturer: Kawasaki Heavy Industries Ltd.

KAWASAKI (Japan)

Model: GPz305

Engine: 4-str sohc parallel twin
Capacity: 306 cc
Bore × Stroke: 61 × 52.4 mm
Compression ratio: 9.7:1
Carburettor: 2/32 mm cv Keihin
Maximum power: 36 bhp (DIN) at 10 000 rpm
Starting: electric

Transmission: 6-speed with Polychain belt drive

Electrics: 12 v CDI ignition with 9 Ah battery

Frame: Duplex tubular cradle

Suspension: Air-adjustable front fork and fully-adjustable rear *Uni-Trak*

Brakes: Twin 210 mm front discs and 160 mm rear drum

Tyres: Front is 90/90–18 51S
Rear is 110/80–18 58S

Dimensions:
Length: 2 130 mm
Width: 745 mm
Wheelbase: 1 355 mm
Clearance: 155 mm
Seat height: 770 mm
Dry weight: 147 kg
Fuel tank: 17 litres

Performance:
Top speed: 165 km/h
Fuel consumption: 5 l/100 km

Features: Tubeless tyres. Positive neutral finder. Box section swing arm.

Manufacturer: Kawasaki Heavy Industries Ltd.

KAWASAKI (Japan)

Model: Z250 Scorpion

Engine: 4-str sohc parallel twin
Capacity: 248 cc
Bore × Stroke: 55 × 52.4 mm
Compression ratio: 10:1
Carburettor: 2/32 mm Keihin
Maximum power: 33 bhp (DIN) at 10 500 rpm
Starting: electric

Transmission: 6-speed with Polychain belt drive

Electrics: 12 v CDI ignition with 9 Ah battery

Frame: Duplex tubular cradle

Suspension: Air-adjustable front fork with fully-adjustable rear *Uni-Trak*

Brakes: 228 mm front disc and 160 mm rear drum

Tyres: Front is 90/90–18 51S
Rear is 110/80–18 58S

Dimensions:
Length: 2 130 mm
Width: 745 mm
Wheelbase: 1 360 mm
Clearance: 155 mm
Seat height: 770 mm
Dry weight: 143.5 kg
Fuel tank: 17 litres

Performance:
Top speed: 160 km/h
Fuel consumption: 5 l/100 km

Features: Tubeless tyres. Box section swing arm.

Manufacturer: Kawasaki Heavy Industries Ltd.

KAWASAKI (Japan)

Model: KLR250

Engine: 4-str LC dohc 4-valve
single
Capacity: 249 cc
Bore × Stroke: 74 × 58 mm
Compression ratio: 11:1
Carburettor: 34 mm cv Keihin
Maximum power: 28 bhp
(DIN) at 9 000 rpm
Starting: kick

Transmission: 6-speed with
chain drive

Electrics: 12 v CDI ignition
with 4 Ah battery

Frame: Tubular single cradle

Suspension: Air-adjustable
leading axle fork and adjustable
rear *Uni-Trak*

Brakes: Drilled front disc and
120 mm rear drum

Tyres: Front is 3.00–21
Rear is 4.60–17

Dimensions:
Length: 2 220 mm
Width: 855 mm
Wheelbase: 1 415 mm
Clearance: 240 mm
Seat height: 855 mm
Dry weight: 118 kg
Fuel tank: 11 litres

Performance:
Top speed: 144 km/h
Fuel consumption: 4 l/100 km

Features: Kawasaki Automatic
Compression Release
mechanism.

Manufacturer: Kawasaki Heavy Industries Ltd.

KAWASAKI (Japan)

Model: AR125B2

Engine: 2-str LC single
Capacity: 123 cc
Bore × Stroke: 55 × 51.8 mm
Compression ratio: 6.5:1
Carburettor: 26 mm Mikuni
Maximum power: 12 bhp
(DIN) at 8 500 rpm
Starting: kick

Transmission: 6-speed with
chain drive

Electrics: 12 v CDI ignition
with 5 Ah battery

Frame: Duplex tubular cradle

Suspension: Leading axle
front fork and rear *Uni-Trak*
system

Brakes: Drilled front disc and
130 mm rear drum

Tyres: Front is 2.75–18
Rear is 3.00–18

Dimensions:
Length: 2 030 mm
Width: 675 mm
Wheelbase: 1 310 mm
Clearance: 170 mm
Seat height: 795 mm
Dry weight: 104 kg
Fuel tank: 11.5 litres

Performance:
Top speed: 118 km/h
Fuel consumption: 3.8 l/100 km

Features: Rotary and Reed
Valve Induction System to
broaden the power band. A3
model is unrestricted (140 km/h).

Manufacturer: Kawasaki Heavy Industries Ltd.

KAWASAKI (Japan)

Model: KH125

Engine: 2-str disc valve single
Capacity: 123 cc
Bore × Stroke: 55 × 51.8 mm
Compression ratio: 7.3:1
Carburettor: 22 mm Mikuni
Maximum power: 12 bhp
(DIN) at 8 000 rpm
Starting: kick

Transmission: 5-speed with
fully-enclosed chain drive

Electrics: 6 v CDI ignition
with 6 Ah battery

Frame: Tubular single cradle

Suspension: Telescopic front
fork with 5-way adjustable twin
rear shocks

Brakes: 210 mm front disc
and 130 mm rear drum

Tyres: Front is 2.75–18 4PR
Rear is 3.00–18 6PR

Dimensions:
Length: 1 925 mm
Width: 745 mm
Wheelbase: 1 260 mm
Clearance: 150 mm
Seat height: 780 mm
Dry weight: 95.5 kg
Fuel tank: 13.5 litres

Performance:
Top speed: 122 km/h
Fuel consumption: 2 l/100 km

Features: KH125EX has cast
wheels.

Manufacturer: Kawasaki Heavy Industries Ltd.

KAWASAKI (Japan)

Model: KE125

Engine: 2-str disc valve single
Capacity: 124 cc
Bore × Stroke: 56 × 50.6 mm
Compression ratio: 7:1
Carburettor: 24 mm Mikuni
Maximum power: 12 bhp
(DIN) at 6 500 rpm
Starting: kick

Transmission: 6-speed with
chain drive

Electrics: 6 v magneto
ignition with 6 Ah battery

Frame: Tubular single cradle

Suspension: Telescopic front
fork with 5-way adjustable twin
rear shocks

Brakes: 120 mm drums
front and rear

Tyres: Front is 2.75–21
Rear is 3.50–18 4PR

Dimensions:
Length: 2 060 mm
Width: 850 mm
Wheelbase: 1 345 mm
Clearance: 250 mm
Seat height: 830 mm
Dry weight: 99 kg
Fuel tank: 9.6 litres

Performance:
Top speed: 106 km/h
Fuel consumption: 4 l/100 km

Features: KE100 model has
10 bhp 99 cc engine.

Manufacturer: Kawasaki Heavy Industries Ltd.

KAWASAKI (Japan)

Model: KH100EX

Engine: 2-str rotary disc valve single
Capacity: 99 cc
Bore × Stroke: 49.5 × 51.8 mm
Compression ratio: 7:1
Carburettor: 19 mm Mikuni
Maximum power: 11.6 bhp (DIN) at 8 000 rpm
Starting: kick

Transmission: 5-speed with chain drive

Electrics: 6 v magneto ignition with 6 Ah battery

Frame: Duplex tubular cradle

Suspension: Telescopic front fork with twin rear 3-way adjustable shocks

Brakes: 250 mm front disc and 110 mm rear drum

Tyres: Front is 2.50–18
Rear is 2.75–18 4PR

Dimensions:
Length: 1 900 mm
Width: 775 mm
Wheelbase: 1 215 mm
Clearance: 155 mm
Seat height: 765 mm
Dry weight: 93 kg
Fuel tank: 10 litres

Performance:
Top speed: 112 km/h
Fuel consumption: 2.5 l/100 km

Features: KC100 Companion is a basic version with fully-enclosed chain, drum brakes and spoke wheels.

Manufacturer: Kawasaki Heavy Industries Ltd.

KAWASAKI (Japan)

Model: AR50

Engine: 2-str reed valve single
Capacity: 49 cc
Bore × Stroke: 39 × 41.6 mm
Compression ratio: 7:1
Carburettor: 14 mm Mikuni
Maximum power: 2.9 bhp
(DIN) at 4 500 rpm
Starting: kick

Transmission: 5-speed with
chain drive

Electrics: 6 v CDI ignition
with 6 Ah battery

Frame: Tubular single cradle

Suspension: Telescopic front
fork with adjustable rear *Uni-Trak* system

Brakes: 190 mm front disc
and 110 mm rear drum

Tyres: Front is 2.50–18
Rear is 2.75–18 4PR

Dimensions:
Length: 1 880 mm
Width: 630 mm
Wheelbase: 1 195 mm
Clearance: 175 mm
Seat height: 785 mm
Dry weight: 78 kg
Fuel tank: 9.6 litres

Performance:
Top speed: 56 km/h
Fuel consumption: 4 l/100 km

Features: AR80 model has
6-speed gearbox, 10 bhp and
65 km/h top speed. Also with
motocross styling AE50/80.

Manufacturer: Kawasaki Heavy Industries Ltd.

LAVERDA (Italy)

Model: RGS1000

Engine: 4-str dohc in-line triple
Capacity: 981 cc
Bore × Stroke: 75 × 74 mm
Compression ratio: 9:1
Carburettor: 3/32 mm Dell'Orto
Maximum power: 75 bhp (DIN) at 8 000 rpm
Starting: electric

Transmission: 5-speed with chain drive

Electrics: Transistorised 12 v ignition with 32 Ah battery

Frame: Duplex tubular cradle

Suspension: Telehydraulic front fork with twin rear *Marzocchi* piggyback shocks

Brakes: 280 mm Brembo triple disc system

Tyres: Front is 100/90V-18
Rear is 120/90V-18

Dimensions:
Length: 2 180 mm
Width: 650 mm
Wheelbase: 1 500 mm
Clearance: ...
Seat height: 780 mm
Dry weight: 244 kg
Fuel tank: 22 litres

Performance:
Top speed: 225 km/h
Fuel consumption: 8 l/100 km

Features: Variations include the Executive, the Corsa and the specially tuned Jota.

Manufacturer: Moto Laverda S.p.A., via Venezia 30, 36042 Breganze (VI), Italy.

LAVERDA (Italy)

125 LB UNO

125 LB UNO CUSTOM

125 LB STRADA

MALAGUTI (Italy)

Model: Strada RGT/50

Engine: 2-str LC disc valve
single
Capacity: 49.9 cc
Bore × Stroke: 38.8 × 42 mm
Compression ratio: 10:1
Carburettor: 12 mm Dell'Orto
Maximum power: 1.4 bhp
(DIN) at 4 300 rpm
Starting: kick

Transmission: 4-speed with
chain drive

Electrics: Flywheel magneto
6 v ignition

Frame: Duplex tubular cradle

Suspension: Telehydraulic
front fork with twin rear shocks

Brakes: Front disc and rear
drum

Tyres: Front is 2.75–16
Rear is 3.00–17

Dimensions:
Length: ...
Width: ...
Wheelbase: ...
Clearance: ...
Seat height: ...
Dry weight: 75 kg
Fuel tank: ...

Performance:
Top speed: 40 km/h
Fuel consumption: 2 l/100 km

Features: ...

Manufacturer: Malaguti S.p.A., via Emilia Levante 498,
40068 San Lazzaro di Savena (BO), Italy.

MALAGUTI (Italy)

Model: Enduro MDX50

Engine: 2-str LC disc valve single
Capacity: 49.9 cc
Bore × Stroke: 38.8 × 42 mm
Compression ratio: 11:1
Carburettor: 12 mm Dell'Orto
Maximum power: 1.36 bhp (DIN) at 5 000 rpm
Starting: kick

Transmission: 4-speed with chain drive

Electrics: Flywheel magneto 6 v ignition

Frame: Duplex tubular cradle

Suspension: Telehydraulic leading axle fork with adjustable rear *Monogas* system

Brakes: Front disc and rear drum

Tyres: Front is 2.75–21
Rear is 3.50–18

Dimensions:
Length: ...
Width: ...
Wheelbase: ...
Clearance: ...
Seat height: ...
Dry weight: 87 kg
Fuel tank: ...

Performance:
Top speed: 40 km/h
Fuel consumption: 2 l/100 km

Features: Other models include RCX/W50 and the Enduro Sahib with a large fuel tank.

Manufacturer: Malaguti S.p.A.

MALANCA (Italy)

Model: OB ONE 6M

Engine: 2-str LC twin
Capacity: 124.9 cc
Bore × Stroke: 43 × 43 mm
Compression ratio: 11:1
Carburettor: 2/22 mm Dell'Orto
Maximum power: 25 bhp
(DIN) at 11 000 rpm
Starting: kick

Transmission: 6-speed with chain drive

Electrics: Flywheel magneto 12 v ignition

Frame: Duplex tubular cradle

Suspension: Telehydraulic front fork with anti-dive and rear monoshock system

Brakes: 220 mm triple disc system

Tyres: Front is 100/90–16
Rear is 100/90–18

Dimensions:
Length: 1 900 mm
Width: 600 mm
Wheelbase: 1 280 mm
Clearance: ...
Seat height: ...
Dry weight: 100 kg
Fuel tank: 13 litres

Performance:
Top speed: 150 km/h
Fuel consumption: 6 l/100 km

Features: Also available with full GP racing fairing.

Manufacturer: Malanca S.p.A., via Pila 6, 40044 Pontecchio di Sasso Marconi (BO), Italy.

MALANCA (Italy)

Model: Mark 125

Engine: 2-str LC twin
Capacity: 124.9 cc
Bore × Stroke: 43 × 43 mm
Compression ratio: 11:1
Carburettor: 2/22 mm Dell'Orto
Maximum power: 18 bhp
(DIN) at 9 000 rpm
Starting: kick

Transmission: 5-speed with
chain drive

Electrics: Flywheel magneto
12 v ignition

Frame: Tubular single cradle

Suspension: Telehydraulic
leading axle fork with rear gas
monoshock system

Manufacturer: Malanca S.p.A.

Brakes: 230 mm front disc
and 125 mm rear drum

Tyres: Front is 2.75–21
Rear is 3.00–18

Dimensions:
Length: 2 100 mm
Width: 800 mm
Wheelbase: 1 400 mm
Clearance: ...
Seat height: ...
Dry weight: 100 kg
Fuel tank: 13 litres

Performance:
Top speed: 120 km/h
Fuel consumption: 6 l/100 km

Features: ...

MALANCA (Italy)

Model: GTS 5 H_2O

Engine: 2-str LC single
Capacity: 49.6 cc
Bore × Stroke: 38.8 × 42 mm
Compression ratio: 9:1
Carburettor: 12 mm Dell'Orto
Maximum power: 1.5 bhp
(DIN) at 5 000 rpm
Starting: electric/kick

Transmission: 5-speed with
chain drive

Electrics: Flywheel magneto
6 v ignition and 8 Ah battery

Frame: Duplex tubular cradle

Suspension: Telescopic front
fork with 3-way adjustable rear
shocks

Manufacturer: Malanca S.p.A.

Brakes: 220 mm front disc
and 118 mm rear drum

Tyres: Front is 2.75–17
Rear is 3.00–17

Dimensions:
Length: ...
Width: 700 mm
Wheelbase: 1 190 mm
Clearance: ...
Seat height: ...
Dry weight: 70 kg
Fuel tank: 10 litres

Performance:
Top speed: 45 km/h
Fuel consumption: 2 l/100 km

Features: Available with 80 cc
engine. Range includes the Due
Piu mopeds.

MOTO GUZZI (Italy)

Model: Le Mans 1000

Engine: 4-str ohv 90° vee-twin
Capacity: 948.8 cc
Bore × Stroke: 88 × 78 mm
Compression ratio: 10:1
Carburettor: 2/40 mm Dell'Orto
Maximum power: 81.5 bhp
(DIN) at 7 400 rpm
Starting: electric

Transmission: 5-speed with
shaft drive

Electrics: Transistorised 12 v
ignition with 24 Ah battery

Frame: Duplex semi-cradle

Suspension: Air-assisted front
fork with twin rear *Koni* gas
shocks

Brakes: 270 mm triple floater
disc system

Tyres: Front is 120/80V–16
Rear is 130/80V–18

Dimensions:
Length: 2 160 mm
Width: 690 mm
Wheelbase: 1 514 mm
Clearance: 120 mm
Seat height: 750 mm
Dry weight: 215 kg
Fuel tank: 25 litres

Performance:
Top speed: 230 km/h
Fuel consumption: 6 l/100 km

Features: Integral braking
system with front and rear disc
operated in balance by the foot
pedal.

Manufacturer: SEIMM Moto Guzzi S.p.A., via E.V. Parodi 57,
22054 Mandello del Lario (CO), Italy.

MOTO GUZZI (Italy)

Model: 1000 SPADA II

Engine: 4-str ohv 90° vee-twin
Capacity: 948.8 cc
Bore × Stroke: 88 × 78 mm
Compression ratio: 9.2:1
Carburettor: 2/30 mm Dell'Orto
Maximum power: 67 bhp
(DIN) at 6 700 rpm
Starting: electric

Transmission: 5-speed with
shaft drive

Electrics: Transistorised 12 v
ignition with 24 Ah battery

Frame: Duplex semi-cradle

Suspension: Air-assisted front
fork with twin rear *Koni* gas
shocks

Brakes: 270 mm triple floater
disc system

Tyres: Front is 110/90V–16
Rear is 120/90V–18

Dimensions:
Length: 2 180 mm
Width: 750 mm
Wheelbase: 1 480 mm
Clearance: 150 mm
Seat height: 750 mm
Dry weight: 220 kg
Fuel tank: 26 litres

Performance:
Top speed: 200 km/h
Fuel consumption: 5.8 l/100 km

Features: Integral braking
system.

Manufacturer: SEIMM Moto Guzzi S.p.A.

MOTO GUZZI (Italy)

Model: California II

Engine: 4-str ohv 90° vee-twin
Capacity: 948.8 cc
Bore × Stroke: 88 × 78 mm
Compression ratio: 9.2:1
Carburettor: 2/30 mm Dell'Orto
Maximum power: 71 bhp
(DIN) at 6 750 rpm
Starting: electric

Transmission: 5-speed with
shaft drive

Electrics: Transistorised 12 v
ignition with 24 Ah battery

Frame: Duplex semi-cradle

Suspension: Telescopic front
fork with twin rear adjustable
shocks

Brakes: Twin 300 mm front
discs and 242 mm rear disc

Tyres: 120/90H–18 front and
rear

Dimensions:
Length: ...
Width: ...
Wheelbase: 1 565 mm
Clearance: ...
Seat height: ...
Dry weight: 250 kg
Fuel tank: 25 litres

Performance:
Top speed: 190 km/h
Fuel consumption: 5.8 l/100 km

Features: American styling
based on the model used by
police departments in
California.

Manufacturer: SEIMM Moto Guzzi S.p.A.

MOTO GUZZI (Italy)

Model: 850–T5

Engine: 4-str ohv 90° vee-twin
Capacity: 844.05 cc
Bore × Stroke: 83 × 78 mm
Compression ratio: 9.5:1
Carburettor: 2/30 mm Dell'Orto
Maximum power: 62 bhp
(DIN) at 6 750 rpm
Starting: electric

Transmission: 5-speed with
shaft drive

Electrics: Transistorised 12 v
ignition with 24 Ah battery

Frame: Duplex semi-cradle

Suspension: Air-assisted front
fork with twin rear gas/oil
shocks

Brakes: Twin 300 mm front
discs and 242 mm rear disc

Tyres: Front is 110/90V–16
Rear is 130/90V–16

Dimensions:
Length: ...
Width: ...
Wheelbase: 1 505 mm
Clearance: ...
Seat height: 750 mm
Dry weight: 220 kg
Fuel tank: 23 litres

Performance:
Top speed: 200 km/h
Fuel consumption: 5.4 l/100 km

Features: Integral braking
system.

Manufacturer: SEIMM Moto Guzzi S.p.A.

MOTO GUZZI (Italy)

Model: V65 Lario

Engine: 4-str ohv 90° 8-valve vee-twin
Capacity: 643.4 cc
Bore × Stroke: 80 × 64 mm
Compression ratio: 10.3:1
Carburettor: 2/30 mm Dell'Orto
Maximum power: 60 bhp
(DIN) at 7 000 rpm
Starting: electric

Transmission: 5-speed with shaft drive

Electrics: Transistorised 12 v ignition with 20 Ah battery

Frame: Duplex semi-cradle

Suspension: Air-assisted front fork with rear 5-way adjustable gas/oil shocks

Brakes: Twin 270 mm front discs and 235 mm rear disc

Tyres: Front is 100/90V–16
Rear is 120/90V–16

Dimensions:
Length: 2 100 mm
Width: 700 mm
Wheelbase: 1 480 mm
Clearance: 140 mm
Seat height: 790 mm
Dry weight: 172 kg
Fuel tank: 18 litres

Performance:
Top speed: Over 195 km/h
Fuel consumption: 5.6 l/100 km

Features: Integral braking system. Series also includes the V65SP and customised V65C.

Manufacturer: SEIMM Moto Guzzi S.p.A.

MOTO GUZZI (Italy)

Model: V65TT

Engine: 4-str ohv 90° vee-twin
Capacity: 643.4 cc
Bore × Stroke: 80 × 64 mm
Compression ratio: 10:1
Carburettor: 2/30 mm Dell'Orto
Maximum power: 50 bhp
(DIN) at 7 250 rpm
Starting: electric

Transmission: 5-speed with
shaft drive

Electrics: Transistorised 12 v
ignition with 20 Ah battery

Frame: Duplex semi-cradle

Suspension: Leading axle fork
with rear adjustable hydraulic
shocks

Brakes: 260 mm discs at front
and rear

Tyres: Front is 3.00–21
Rear is 4.00–18

Dimensions:
Length: ...
Width: ...
Wheelbase: 1 480 mm
Clearance: ...
Seat height: ...
Dry weight: 165 kg
Fuel tank: 16 litres

Performance:
Top speed: Over 160 km/h
Fuel consumption: 5.4 l/100 km

Features: TT is 'Tutto
Terreno'. Series includes the
V35TT with 31 bhp 350 cc
motor.

Manufacturer: SEIMM Moto Guzzi S.p.A.

MOTO GUZZI (Italy)

Model: V50 Monza II

Engine: 4-str ohv 90° 8-valve
vee-twin
Capacity: 490.29 cc
Bore × Stroke: 74 × 57 mm
Compression ratio: 10.4:1
Carburettor: 2/30 mm Dell'Orto
Maximum power: 50 bhp
(DIN) at 7 800 rpm
Starting: electric

Transmission: 5-speed with
shaft drive

Electrics: Transistorised 12 v
ignition with 20 Ah battery

Frame: Tubular cradle

Suspension: Air-assisted front
fork with twin rear adjustable
gas/oil shocks

Brakes: Twin 270 mm front
discs and 235 mm rear disc

Tyres: Front is 100/90V–16
Rear is 120/90V–16

Dimensions:
Length: 2 090 mm
Width: 700 mm
Wheelbase: 1 455 mm
Clearance: 175 mm
Seat height: 775 mm
Dry weight: 170 kg
Fuel tank: 18 litres

Performance:
Top speed: over 185 km/h
Fuel consumption: 5.2 l/100 km

Features: Integral brake
system. V50III is standard
model.

Manufacturer: SEIMM Moto Guzzi S.p.A.

MOTO GUZZI (Italy)

Model: V35 Imola II

Engine: 4-str ohv 90° 8-valve
vee-twin
Capacity: 346.22 cc
Bore × Stroke: 66 × 50.6 mm
Compression ratio: 10.5:1
Carburettor: 2/28 mm Dell'Orto
Maximum power: 40 bhp
(DIN) at 8 800 rpm
Starting: electric

Transmission: 5-speed with
shaft drive

Electrics: Transistorised 12 v
ignition with 20 Ah battery

Frame: Tubular cradle

Suspension: Air-assisted front
fork with twin rear adjustable
gas/oil shocks

Brakes: Twin 270 mm front
discs and 235 mm rear disc

Tyres: Front is 100/90V–16
Rear is 120/90V–16

Dimensions:
Length: 2 090 mm
Width: 700 mm
Wheelbase: 1 455 mm
Clearance: 175 mm
Seat height: 775 mm
Dry weight: 168 kg
Fuel tank: 18 litres

Performance:
Top speed: 170 km/h
Fuel consumption: 4.8 l/100 km

Features: Integral brake
system. Series includes
standard V35II and custom
V35C.

Manufacturer: SEIMM Moto Guzzi S.p.A.

MOTO MORINI (Italy)

Model: 501 Camel

Engine: 4-str ohv 72° vee-twin
Capacity: 507 cc
Bore × Stroke: 71 × 64 mm
Compression ratio: 11.5:1
Carburettor: 2/28 mm Dell'Orto
Maximum power: 43 bhp
(DIN) at 8 500 rpm
Starting: kick

Transmission: 6-speed with
chain drive

Electrics: 6 v CDI ignition
with 2 Ah battery

Frame: Duplex box cradle

Suspension: Leading axle fork
with rear adjustable monoshock
system

Brakes: 260 mm front disc
and 230 mm rear disc

Tyres: Front is 3.00–21
Rear is 4.00–18

Dimensions:
Length: 2 270 mm
Width: ...
Wheelbase: 1 470 mm
Clearance: 300 mm
Seat height: 880 mm
Dry weight: 154 kg
Fuel tank: 14 litres

Performance:
Top speed: 163 km/h
Fuel consumption: 5 l/100 km

Features: Series includes
350 cc version named
Kangeroo.

Manufacturer: Moto Morini (Fabbrica Italiana Motocicli S.p.A.),
via A. Bergami 7, 40133 Bologna, Italy.

MOTO MORINI (Italy)

Model: 350K2

Engine: 4-str ohv 72° vee-twin
Capacity: 344.16 cc
Bore × Stroke: 62 × 57 mm
Compression ratio: 11:1
Carburettor: 2/25 mm Dell'Orto
Maximum power: 35 bhp
(DIN) at 8 500 rpm
Starting: electric/kick

Transmission: 6-speed with
chain drive

Electrics: 12 v CDI ignition
with 18 Ah battery

Frame: Duplex tubular cradle

Suspension: Telehydraulic
fork with twin rear adjustable
hydraulic shocks

Brakes: Twin 260 mm front
discs and 240 mm rear disc

Tyres: Front is 100/90V–18
Rear is 3.50H–18

Dimensions:
Length: 2 080 mm
Width: ...
Wheelbase: 1 390 mm
Clearance: 170 mm
Seat height: 800 mm
Dry weight: 160 kg
Fuel tank: 16 litres

Performance:
Top speed: 160 km/h
Fuel consumption: 3.7 l/100 km

Features: Other Morini
models in 125 cc and 500 cc
versions.

Manufacturer: Moto Morini S.p.A.

MOTO MORINI (Italy)

Model: 125KJ

Engine: 4-str single
Capacity: 123 cc
Bore × Stroke: 59 × 45 mm
Compression ratio: 11.7:1
Carburettor: 24 mm Dell'Orto
Maximum power: 12.5 bhp
(DIN) at 10 000 rpm
Starting: kick

Transmission: 6-speed with
chain drive

Electrics: 6 v CDI ignition
with 2 Ah battery

Frame: Tubular single cradle

Suspension: Leading axle fork
with adjustable rear monoshock
system

Manufacturer: Moto Morini S.p.A.

Brakes: 230 mm front disc
and 136 mm rear drum

Tyres: Front is 3.00–21
Rear is 4.10–18

Dimensions:
Length: 2 150 mm
Width: ...
Wheelbase: 1 390 mm
Clearance: 280 mm
Seat height: 840 mm
Dry weight: 112 kg
Fuel tank: 7.5 litres

Performance:
Top speed: 110 km/h
Fuel consumption: 2.9 l/100 km

Features: ...

MZ (East Germany)

Model: ETZ150

Engine: 2-str piston port single
Capacity: 143 cc
Bore × Stroke: 56 × 58 mm
Compression ratio: 10.5:1
Carburettor: 22 mm BVF
Maximum power: 13.5 bhp (DIN) at 6 000 rpm
Starting: kick

Transmission: 5-speed with fully enclosed chain drive

Electrics: 12 v coil ignition with 5 Ah battery

Frame: Welded spine

Suspension: Telescopic front fork with twin rear 3-way adjustable shocks

Brakes: 280 mm front disc and 150 mm rear drum

Tyres: Front is 2.75–18
Rear is 3.00–18

Dimensions:
Length: 1 980 mm
Width: 805 mm
Wheelbase: 1 175 mm
Clearance: ...
Seat height ...
Dry weight: 106 kg
Fuel tank: 13 litres

Performance:
Top speed: 110 km/h
Fuel consumption: 3 l/100 km

Features: Series includes 125 cc and 250 cc versions. The larger 21 bhp machine is also sold with a sidecar fitted.

Manufacturer: VEB Motorradwerk, Neue Mariemberger Str. 189, Zschopau–936, DDR (East Germany).

NEVAL (USSR)

Model: Ural M67

Engine: 4-str ohv flat twin
Capacity: 649 cc
Bore × Stroke: 78 × 68 mm
Compression ratio: 7.2:1
Carburettor: 2/K301
Maximum power: 36 bhp
(DIN) at 5 300 rpm
Starting: side kick

Transmission: 4-speed with
shaft drive and neutral lever

Electrics: 12 v coil ignition
with battery and dynamo

Frame: Duplex tubular cradle

Suspension: Telescopic front
fork with twin rear 2-way
adjustable shocks

Brakes: Drums at front and
rear

Tyres: 3.50–18 at front and
rear

Dimensions:
Length: ...
Width: ...
Wheelbase: 1 500 mm
Clearance: ...
Seat height: ...
Dry weight: 215 kg
Fuel tank: 18 litres

Performance:
Top speed: 150 km/h
Fuel consumption: 6 l/100 km

Features: Comes with solo or
dual saddle, crash bars and 34
piece tool/spares set.

Exported by: Avtoexport—14, Volkhonka Street—119902,
Moscow, USSR

NEVAL (USSR)

Model: Electronic 125

Engine: 2-str piston port
single
Capacity: 123 cc
Bore × Stroke: 52 × 58 mm
Compression ratio: 9:1
Carburettor: ...
Maximum power: 11 bhp
(DIN) at 6 500 rpm
Starting: kick

Transmission: 4-speed with
chain drive

Electrics: 6 v electronic
ignition and direct lighting

Frame: Tubular single cradle

Suspension: Telehydraulic
fork with twin rear 2-way
adjustable hydraulic shocks

Exported by: Avtoexport.

Brakes: 160 mm drums front
and rear

Tyres: 3.00–18 front and rear

Dimensions:
Length: ...
Width: ...
Wheelbase: 1 275 mm
Clearance: ...
Seat height: ...
Dry weight: 100 kg
Fuel tank: 11.5 litres

Performance:
Top speed: 95 km/h
Fuel consumption: 3 l/100 km

Features: Derived from
MMV2 Minsk 3.

NORTON (UK)

Photo: Courtesy of West Midlands Police

Model: Interpol 2

Engine: Twin chamber Wankel
rotary
Capacity: 588 cc
Bore × Stroke: ...
Compression ratio: 8.2:1
Carburettor: 2/38 mm SU
Maximum power: 75 bhp
(DIN) at 8 500 rpm
Starting: electric

Transmission: 5-speed with
chain drive

Electrics: Transistorised 12 v
ignition with 14 Ah battery

Frame: Sheet steel box

Suspension: Telehydraulic
fork with twin rear 3-way
adjustable *Girling* shocks

Brakes: 280 mm triple disc
system with d-pc

Tyres: Front is 4.10V–18
Rear is 4.25/85V–18

Dimensions:
Length: 1 805 mm
Width: 710 mm
Wheelbase: 1 486 mm
Clearance: 165 mm
Seat height: 762 mm
Dry weight: 260 kg
Fuel tank: 24 litres

Performance:
Top speed: ...
Fuel consumption: ...

Features: Detachable full
fairing and full police
specification.

Manufacturer: Norton Motors (1978) Ltd., Lynn Lane, Shenstone,
Lichfield, Staffs WS14 0EA, England.

PIAGGIO (Italy)

Model: Vespa Arcobalena

Engine: 2-str rotary disc valve single
Capacity: 197.9 cc
Bore × Stroke: 66.5 × 57 mm
Compression ratio: 8.8:1
Carburettor: 24 mm Dell'Orto
Maximum power: 11.6 bhp (DIN) at 6 000 rpm
Starting: kick/electric

Transmission: 4-speed with direct drive to rear wheel

Electrics: Transistorised 6 v ignition

Frame: Monocoque

Suspension: Variable pitch helical springs with double action shocks

Brakes: 150 mm drums front and rear

Tyres: 3.50–10 front and rear

Dimensions:
Length: 1 760 mm
Width: 695 mm
Wheelbase: 1 235 mm
Clearance: 200 mm
Seat height: 790 mm
Dry weight: 108 kg
Fuel tank: 8 litres

Performance:
Top speed: 110 km/h
Fuel consumption: 2.1 l/100 km

Features: There are many Vespa models: PX80E, 125E, 150E, 200E, the PK125S automatic and the PK50 electronic.

Manufacturer: Piaggio & Co S.p.A., via Antonio Cecchi 6, 16129, Genova, Italy.

PIAGGIO (Italy)

Model: Bravo PV

Engine: 2-str horizontal single
Capacity: 49.2 cc
Bore × Stroke: 38.2 × 43 mm
Compression ratio: 8.9:1
Carburettor: 12 mm Dell'Orto
Maximum power: 1.4 bhp
(DIN) at 4 500 rpm
Starting: pedal

Transmission: Single speed
with automatic clutch

Electrics: 6 v flywheel
magneto ignition

Frame: Tubular spine

Suspension: Telescopic front
fork with adjustable mechanical
rear dampers

Manufacturer: Piaggio & Co S.p.A.

Brakes: 90 mm front drum
and 136 mm rear drum

Tyres: 2.25–16
front and rear

Dimensions:
Length: 1 595 mm
Width: 675 mm
Wheelbase: 1 050 mm
Clearance: ...
Seat height: adj.
Dry weight: 48.2 kg
Fuel tank: 3 litres

Performance:
Top speed: 39 km/h
Fuel consumption: 1.5 l/100 km

Features: P version without
the gear variations.

PIAGGIO (Italy)

Model: Ciao PXV

Engine: 2-str horizontal single
Capacity: 49.28 cc
Bore × Stroke: 38.4 × 43 mm
Compression ratio: 9:1
Carburettor: 10 mm Dell'Orto
Maximum power: 1.4 bhp
(DIN) at 4 500 rpm
Starting: pedal

Transmission: Single speed
with automatic clutch

Electrics: 6 v flywheel
magneto ignition

Frame: Step-thru

Suspension: Front rocker arm
with under saddle springing

Manufacturer: Piaggio & Co S.p.A.

Brakes: 90 mm front drum
and 136 mm rear drum

Tyres: 2.00–17
front and rear

Dimensions:
Length: 1 570 mm
Width: 630 mm
Wheelbase: 1 025 mm
Clearance: ...
Seat height: adj.
Dry weight: 39 kg
Fuel tank: 2.8 litres

Performance:
Top speed: 39 km/h
Fuel consumption: 1.4 l/100 km

Features: ...

PUCH (Austria)

Model: Lady

Engine: 2-str piston port
single
Capacity: 48.8 cc
Bore × Stroke: 38 × 43 mm
Compression ratio: 9:1
Carburettor: 14 mm Bing
Maximum power: 2.25 bhp
(DIN) at 5 000 rpm
Starting: kick

Transmission: Single speed
with automatic clutch

Electrics: 6 v flywheel
magneto ignition

Frame: Pressed steel spine

Suspension: Telescopic front
fork with twin rear dampers

Brakes: 80 mm drums front
and rear

Tyres: 2.50–14
front and rear

Dimensions:
Length: 1 650 mm
Width: 680 mm
Wheelbase: 1 100 mm
Clearance: 130 mm
Seat height: ...
Dry weight: 48 kg
Fuel tank: 3.8 litres

Performance:
Top speed: 48 km/h
Fuel consumption:
1.98 l/100 km

Features: Other models
include the Maxi Plus and Maxi
Supreme.

Manufacturer: Steyr-Daimler-Puch AG-Bereich-8011 Graz,
Austria.

SIMSON (East Germany)

Model: S70E/2

Engine: 2-str piston port
single
Capacity: 70 cc
Bore × Stroke: 44 × 45 mm
Compression ratio: 10.5:1
Carburettor: 16 mm BVF
Maximum power: 5.6 bhp
(DIN) at 6 000 rpm
Starting: kick

Transmission: 4-speed with
chain drive

Electrics: Transistorised 6 v
ignition with 12 Ah battery

Frame: Single spine

Suspension: Telescopic front
fork with twin rear hydraulic
shocks

Brakes: 125 mm drums front
and rear

Tyres: 2.75–16
front and rear

Dimensions:
Length: 1 890 mm
Width: 635 mm
Wheelbase: 1 210 mm
Clearance: 130 mm
Seat height: 760 mm
Dry weight: 84 kg
Fuel tank: 8.7 litres

Performance:
Top speed: 75 km/h
Fuel consumption: 2.6 l/100 km

Features: S70 is standard
road model.

Manufacturer: Simson (IFA Kombinat) DDR–6000 Suhl, PSF 209.

SIMSON (East Germany)

Model: S51 B2-4/1

Engine: 2-str piston port single
Capacity: 49.8 cc
Bore × Stroke: 38 × 44 mm
Compression ratio: 9.5:1
Carburettor: 16 mm BVF
Maximum power: 3.7 bhp (DIN) at 5 500 rpm
Starting: kick

Transmission: 4-speed with chain drive

Electrics: Transistorised 6 v ignition with 12 Ah battery

Frame: Single spine

Suspension: Telescopic front fork with twin rear hydraulic shocks

Brakes: 125 mm drums front and rear

Tyres: 2.75–16 front and rear

Dimensions:
Length: 1 890 mm
Width: 635 mm
Wheelbase: 1 210 mm
Clearance: 130 mm
Seat height: 760 mm
Dry weight: 78.5 kg
Fuel tank: 8.7 litres

Performance:
Top speed: 40–60 km/h
Fuel consumption: 2.5 l/100 km

Features: Retractable kick starter. Enclosed chain. S51 is a 3-speed version.

Manufacturer: Simson (IFA Kombinat).

SUZUKI (Japan)

Model: GSX1100EF

Engine: 4-str dohc 16-valve
in-line four
Capacity: 1 135 cc
Bore × Stroke: 74 × 66 mm
Compression ratio: 9.7:1
Carburettor: 4/36 mm Mikuni
Maximum power: 122 bhp
(DIN) at 8 500 rpm
Starting: electric

Transmission: 5-speed with
chain drive

Electrics: Transistorised 12 v
ignition with 14 Ah battery

Frame: Box section cradle

Suspension: Telescopic fork
with *PDF* anti-dive and
remotely adjustable rear *Full-
Floater* system

Brakes: Triple disc system
with d-pc

Tyres: Front is 110/90V–16
Rear is 130/90V–17

Dimensions:
Length: 2 240 mm
Width: 815 mm
Wheelbase: 1 550 mm
Clearance: 155 mm
Seat height: 785 mm
Dry weight: 232 kg
Fuel tank: 20 litres

Performance:
Top speed: 250 km/h
Fuel consumption: 7.2 l/100 km

Features: Positive Damping
Force system controls front
suspension. GSX range
flagship.

Manufacturer: Suzuki Motor Co. Ltd., Hamamatsu-Nishi
P.O. Box 1, 432–91, Hamamatsu, Japan.

SUZUKI (Japan)

Model: GSX1100S

Engine: 4-str dohc 16-valve
in-line four
Capacity: 1 074 cc
Bore × Stroke: 72 × 66 mm
Compression ratio: 9.5:1 .
Carburettor: 4/34 mm Mikuni
Maximum power: 111 bhp
(SAE) at 8 500 rpm
Starting: electric

Transmission: 5-speed with
chain drive

Electrics: Transistorised 12 v
ignition with 14 Ah battery

Frame: Duplex tubular cradle

Suspension: Telehydraulic
fork with anti-dive and twin
rear adjustable shocks

Manufacturer: Suzuki Motor Co. Ltd.

Brakes: 280 mm triple disc
system

Tyres: Front is 3.50V–19
Rear is 4.50V–17

Dimensions:
Length: . . .
Width: 930 mm
Wheelbase: 1 525 mm
Clearance: 175 mm
Seat height: 775 mm
Dry weight: 232 kg
Fuel tank: 21 litres

Performance:
Top speed: 232 km/h
Fuel consumption: 6.5 l/100 km

Features: Top model during
the Katana styling period.

SUZUKI (Japan)

Model: XN85

Engine: 4-str dohc turbo four
Capacity: 673 cc
Bore × Stroke: 62 × 55.8 mm
Compression ratio: 7.4:1
Carburettor: fuel injection
Maximum power: 85 bhp
(DIN) at 8 500 rpm
Starting: electric

Transmission: 5-speed with
chain drive

Electrics: Transistorised 12 v
ignition with 14 Ah battery

Frame: Duplex tubular cradle

Suspension: Telescopic front
fork with anti-dive and rear *Full-
Floater* system

Brakes: Triple disc system

Tyres: Front is 100/90H–16
Rear is 120/90H–17

Dimensions:
Length: 2 150 mm
Width: 725 mm
Wheelbase: 1 490 mm
Clearance: 145 mm
Seat height: 770 mm
Dry weight: 230 kg
Fuel tank: 19 litres

Performance:
Top speed: 206 km/h
Fuel consumption: 7 l/100 km

Features: Katana styling.

Manufacturer: Suzuki Motor Co. Ltd.

SUZUKI (Japan)

Model: GS850G

Engine: 4-str dohc in-line four
Capacity: 843 cc
Bore × Stroke: 69 × 56.4 mm
Compression ratio: 8.8:1
Carburettor: 4/32 mm Mikuni
Maximum power: 80 bhp
(DIN) at 8 500 rpm
Starting: electric

Transmission: 5-speed with shaft drive

Electrics: Transistorised 12 v ignition with 14 Ah battery

Frame: Duplex tubular cradle

Suspension: Telescopic front forks with twin rear 4-way adjustable hydraulic shocks

Brakes: 280 mm triple disc system

Tyres: Front is 3.50H–19
Rear is 4.50H–19

Dimensions:
Length: 2 195 mm
Width: 865 mm
Wheelbase: 1 500 mm
Clearance: 170 mm
Seat height: 810 mm
Dry weight: 243 kg
Fuel tank: 22 litres

Performance:
Top speed: 205 km/h
Fuel consumption: 6.8 l/100 km

Features: Tubeless tyres fitted.
Also as GS650GT with 673 cc,
65 bhp motor.

Manufacturer: Suzuki Motor Co. Ltd.

SUZUKI (Japan)

Model: GSXR750

Engine: 4-str LC dohc TSCC
in-line four
Capacity: 749 cc
Bore × Stroke: 70 × 48.7 mm
Compression ratio: 10.6:1
Carburettor: 4/29 mm Mikuni
Maximum power: 100 bhp
(DIN) at 10 500 rpm
Starting: electric

Transmission: 6-speed with
chain drive

Electrics: Transistorised 12 v
ignition with 14 Ah battery

Frame: Aluminium box section

Suspension: Telescopic front
fork 4-way adjustable and rear
Full-Floater system

Brakes: Triple disc system

Tyres: Front is 110/80V–18
Rear is 140/70V–18

Dimensions:
Length: 2 105 mm
Width: 745 mm
Wheelbase: 1 435 mm
Clearance: 120 mm
Seat height: 770 mm
Dry weight: 176 kg
Fuel tank: 19 litres

Performance:
Top speed: 240 km/h
Fuel consumption: 7 l/100 km

Features: Twin Swirl
Combustion Chambers. Oil
cooled 16-valve engine. Anti-
dive fork.

Manufacturer: Suzuki Motor Co. Ltd.

SUZUKI (Japan)

Model: GSX750ES

Engine: 4-str dohc TSCC
16-valve four
Capacity: 747 cc
Bore × Stroke: 67 × 53 mm
Compression ratio: 9.6:1
Carburettor: 4/32 mm Mikuni
Maximum power: 83 bhp
(DIN) at 9 500 rpm
Starting: electric

Transmission: 5-speed with
chain drive

Electrics: Transistorised 12 v
ignition with 14 Ah battery

Frame: Box section cradle

Suspension: Telescopic front
fork with anti-dive and rear
remotely adjustable *Full-Floater*

Brakes: Triple disc system
with d-pc

Tyres: Front is 120/80V–16
Rear is 130/80V–18

Dimensions:
Length: 2 200 mm
Width: 735 mm
Wheelbase: 1 510 mm
Clearance: 140 mm
Seat height: 785 mm
Dry weight: 215 kg
Fuel tank: 19.5 litres

Performance:
Top speed: 210 km/h
Fuel consumption: 7 l/100 km

Features: Twin Swirl
Combustion Chambers. EF
model has full fairing.

Manufacturer: Suzuki Motor Co. Ltd.

SUZUKI (Japan)

Model: DR600 Raider

Engine: 4-str sohc TSCC
4-valve single
Capacity: 589 cc
Bore × Stroke: 94 × 85 mm
Compression ratio: 8.5:1
Carburettor: 38 mm Mikuni
Maximum power: 44 bhp
(DIN) at 6 500 rpm
Starting: kick

Transmission: 5-speed with
chain drive

Electrics: Transistorised 12 v
ignition with 5 Ah battery

Frame: Tubular cradle

Suspension: Air-assisted
leading axle fork with 5-way
adjustable rear *Full-Floater*

Brakes: Front disc and rear
drum

Tyres: Front is 100/80–21
Rear is 130/80–17

Dimensions:
Length: 2 215 mm
Width: 875 mm
Wheelbase: 1 465 mm
Clearance: 275 mm
Seat height: 870 mm
Dry weight: 139 kg
Fuel tank: 21 litres

Performance:
Top speed: 160 km/h
Fuel consumption: 6 l/100 km

Features: Twin Swirl
Combustion Chambers and
automatic decompressor. Paris–
Dakar rally styling.

Manufacturer: Suzuki Motor Co. Ltd.

SUZUKI (Japan)

Model: GSX550ES

Engine: 4-str dohc TSCC
16-valve four
Capacity: 572 cc
Bore × Stroke: 60 × 50.6 mm
Compression ratio: 9.8:1
Carburettor: 2/30 mm Mikuni
Maximum power: 61 bhp
(DIN) at 9 500 rpm
Starting: electric

Transmission: 6-speed with
chain drive

Electrics: Transistorised 12 v
ignition with 12 Ah battery

Frame: Box section cradle

Suspension: Telescopic front
fork with anti-dive and rear
Full-Floater system

Brakes: Triple disc system

Tyres: Front is 100/90H–16
Rear is 110/90H–18

Dimensions:
Length: 2 120 mm
Width: 770 mm
Wheelbase: 1 420 mm
Clearance: 155 mm
Seat height: 785 mm
Dry weight: 194 kg
Fuel tank: 18 litres

Performance:
Top speed: 200 km/h
Fuel consumption: 6.2 l/100 km

Features: Tubeless tyres.
GSX550EF features a full
fairing.

Manufacturer: Suzuki Motor Co. Ltd.

SUZUKI (Japan)

Model: RG500 Gamma

Engine: 2-str LC disc valve
square four
Capacity: 498 cc
Bore × Stroke: 56 × 50.6 mm
Compression ratio: 7:1
Carburettor: 4/28 mm Mikuni
Maximum power: 95 bhp
(DIN) at 9 500 rpm
Starting: kick

Transmission: 6-speed with
chain drive

Electrics: Transistorised 12 v
ignition with 4 Ah battery

Frame: Aluminium box section

Suspension: Telescopic front
forks with anti-dive and rear
Full-Floater system

Brakes: Triple disc system
with d-pc

Tyres: Front is 110/90V–16
Rear is 120/90V–17

Dimensions:
Length: 2 100 mm
Width: 695 mm
Wheelbase: 1 425 mm
Clearance: 110 mm
Seat height: 800 mm
Dry weight: 154 kg
Fuel tank: 22 litres

Performance:
Top speed: 245 km/h
Fuel consumption: 12 l/100 km

Features: Suzuki Automatic
Exhaust Control system. Power
valve and race instrumentation.

Manufacturer: Suzuki Motor Co. Ltd.

SUZUKI (Japan)

Model: GSX400FZ

Engine: 4-str dohc 16-valve
in-line four
Capacity: 398 cc
Bore × Stroke: 53 × 45.2 mm
Compression ratio: 10.2:1
Carburettor: 4/26 mm Mikuni
Maximum power: 42 bhp
(DIN) at 9 500 rpm
Starting: electric

Transmission: 6-speed with
chain drive

Electrics: Transistorised 12 v
ignition with 12 Ah battery

Frame: Duplex tubular cradle

Suspension: Telescopic front
fork with anti-dive and 5-way
rear hydraulic shocks

Manufacturer: Suzuki Motor Co. Ltd.

Brakes: Triple disc system

Tyres: Front is 3.25S–19
Rear is 3.75S–18

Dimensions:
Length: 2 105 mm
Width: 750 mm
Wheelbase: 1 415 mm
Clearance: 165 mm
Seat height: 780 mm
Dry weight: 179 kg
Fuel tank: 15 litres

Performance:
Top speed: 170 km/h
Fuel consumption: 5.3 l/100
km

Features: ...

SUZUKI (Japan)

Model: RG250 Gamma

Engine: 2-str LC Power Reed twin
Capacity: 247 cc
Bore × Stroke: 54 × 54 mm
Compression ratio: 7:1
Carburettor: 2/28 mm Mikuni
Maximum power: 49 bhp (DIN) at 9 500 rpm
Starting: kick

Transmission: 6-speed with chain drive

Electrics: Transistorised 12 v ignition with 5 Ah battery

Frame: Aluminium box section

Suspension: Telescopic front fork with anti-dive and rear *Full-Floater* system

Brakes: Twin front discs with d-pc and rear disc

Tyres: Front is 100/90–16
Rear is 110/80–18

Dimensions:
Length: 2 050 mm
Width: 685 mm
Wheelbase: 1 385 mm
Clearance: 155 mm
Seat height: 770 mm
Dry weight: 132 kg
Fuel tank: 17 litres

Performance:
Top speed: 193 km/h
Fuel consumption: 6.8 l/100 km

Features: Race style instrumentation. Automatic Exhaust Control System fitted.

Manufacturer: Suzuki Motor Co. Ltd.

SUZUKI (Japan)

Model: RG125 Gamma

Engine: 2-str LC Power Reed
single
Capacity: 123 cc
Bore × Stroke: 54 × 54 mm
Compression ratio: 7.4:1
Carburettor: 28 mm Mikuni
Maximum power: 25 bhp
(DIN) at 9 500 rpm
Starting: kick

Transmission: 6-speed with
chain drive

Electrics: Transistorised 12 v
ignition with 4 Ah battery

Frame: Steel box section

Suspension: Telescopic front
fork with rear adjustable *Full-
Floater* system

Brakes: Front disc and rear
drum

Tyres: Front is 80/100–16
Rear is 90/90–18

Dimensions:
Length: 1 960 mm
Width: 650 mm
Wheelbase: 1 310 mm
Clearance: 145 mm
Seat height: 720 mm
Dry weight: 94 kg
Fuel tank: 13 litres

Performance:
Top speed: 160 km/h
Fuel consumption: ...

Features: UK model (12 bhp)
has exhaust restrictor.
Automatic Exhaust Control
System fitted.

Manufacturer: Suzuki Motor Co. Ltd.

SUZUKI (Japan)

Model: TS125X

Engine: 2-str LC reed valve single
Capacity: 124 cc
Bore × Stroke: 50 × 50.6 mm
Compression ratio: 7.5:1
Carburettor: 24 mm Mikuni
Maximum power: 22 bhp (DIN) at 8 000 rpm
Starting: kick

Transmission: 6-speed with chain drive

Electrics: Transistorised 12 v ignition with 4 Ah battery

Frame: Semi-double cradle

Suspension: Hydraulic leading link fork with rear 5-way adjustable *Full-Floater*

Manufacturer: Suzuki Motor Co. Ltd.

Brakes: 230 mm front disc and rear drum

Tyres: Front is 80/80–21
Rear is 110/80–18

Dimensions:
Length: 2 085 mm
Width: 830 mm
Wheelbase: 1 355 mm
Clearance: 290 mm
Seat height: 890 mm
Dry weight: 105 kg
Fuel tank: 9 litres

Performance:
Top speed: 115 km/h
Fuel consumption: ...

Features: Power Reed intake system. Styled on works motocross team. Also available as TSX250X.

SUZUKI (Japan)

Model: GS125ES

Engine: 4-str ohc single
Capacity: 124 cc
Bore × Stroke: 57 × 48.8 mm
Compression ratio: 9.5:1
Carburettor: 24 mm Mikuni
Maximum power: 12 bhp
(DIN) at 9 500 rpm
Starting: electric

Transmission: 5-speed with
chain drive

Electrics: Transistorised 12 v
ignition with 8 Ah battery

Frame: Tubular single cradle

Suspension: Telescopic front
fork with rear 5-way adjustable
hydraulic shocks

Brakes: Front disc and rear
drum

Tyres: Front is 2.75–18
Rear is 3.00–18

Dimensions:
Length: 1 945 mm
Width: 710 mm
Wheelbase: 1 270 mm
Clearance: 170 mm
Seat height: 745 mm
Dry weight: 103 kg
Fuel tank: 11 litres

Performance:
Top speed: 115 km/h
Fuel consumption: 3.4 l/100 km

Features: Standard model
without fairing and with front
drum brake and spoked wheels
is the GS125.

Manufacturer: Suzuki Motor Co. Ltd.

SUZUKI (Japan)

Model: DR125S

Engine: 4-str sohc single
Capacity: 124 cc
Bore × Stroke: 57 × 48.8 mm
Compression ratio: 9.5:1
Carburettor: 24 mm Mikuni
Maximum power: 12 bhp
(DIN) at 9 500 rpm
Starting: kick

Transmission: 6-speed with
chain drive

Electrics: Transistorised 6 v
ignition with 4 Ah battery

Frame: Semi-double cradle

Suspension: Telehydraulic
front fork with rear *Full-Floater*
system

Brakes: Front disc and rear
drum

Tyres: Front is 80/80–21
Rear is 100/80–18

Dimensions:
Length: 2 170 mm
Width: 845 mm
Wheelbase: 1 390 mm
Clearance: 255 mm
Seat height: 820 mm
Dry weight: 103 kg
Fuel tank: 12 litres

Performance:
Top speed: 110 km/h
Fuel consumption: 3 l/100 km

Features: Trail bike based on
the GS125 roadster.

Manufacturer: Suzuki Motor Co. Ltd.

SUZUKI (Japan)

Model: GP125N

Engine: 2-str disc valve single
Capacity: 123 cc
Bore × Stroke: 56 × 50 mm
Compression ratio: 6.7:1
Carburettor: 24 mm Mikuni
Maximum power: 12 bhp
(DIN) at 8 500 rpm
Starting: kick

Transmission: 5-speed with
chain drive

Electrics: 6 v flywheel
magneto ignition with 4 Ah
battery

Frame: Tubular single cradle

Suspension: Telescopic front
fork with twin rear adjustable
shocks

Brakes: 240 mm front disc
and 140 mm rear drum

Tyres: Front is 2.75–18
Rear is 3.00–18

Dimensions:
Length: 1 895 mm
Width: 750 mm
Wheelbase: 1 230 mm
Clearance: 140 mm
Seat height: 750 mm
Dry weight: 92 kg
Fuel tank: 9.8 litres

Performance:
Top speed: 112 km/h
Fuel consumption: 4 l/100 km

Features: Larger engined
version of GP100.

Manufacturer: Suzuki Motor Co. Ltd.

SUZUKI (Japan)

Model: TS100ERZ

Engine: 2-str reed valve single
Capacity: 98 cc
Bore × Stroke: 50 × 50 mm
Compression ratio: 6.8:1
Carburettor: 22 mm Mikuni
Maximum power: 11 bhp
(DIN) at 11 000 rpm
Starting: kick

Transmission: 5-speed with
chain drive

Electrics: Transistorised 12 v
ignition with 4 Ah battery

Frame: Semi-double cradle

Suspension: Leading axle fork
with rear 5-way adjustable *Full-Floater* system

Manufacturer: Suzuki Motor Co. Ltd.

Brakes: Drums at front and
rear

Tyres: Front is 2.50–21
Rear is 3.00–18

Dimensions:
Length: 2 050 mm
Width: 850 mm
Wheelbase: 1 330 mm
Clearance: 230 mm
Seat height: 780 mm
Dry weight: 90 kg
Fuel tank: 9 litres

Performance:
Top speed: 100 km/h
Fuel consumption: 4 l/100 km

Features: Full size trial bike
also made with smaller engine
(TS50X).

SUZUKI (Japan)

Model: GP100E

Engine: 2-str disc valve single
Capacity: 98 cc
Bore × Stroke: 50 × 50 mm
Compression ratio: 6.8:1
Carburettor: 22 mm Mikuni
Maximum power: 12 bhp
(DIN) at 8 500 rpm
Starting: kick

Transmission: 5-speed with
chain drive

Electrics: 6 v flywheel
magneto ignition with 4 Ah
battery

Frame: Tubular single cradle

Suspension: Telescopic front
fork with twin rear 5-way
adjustable shocks

Manufacturer: Suzuki Motor Co. Ltd.

Brakes: Single discs at front
and rear

Tyres: Front is 2.50–18
Rear is 2.75–18

Dimensions:
Length: 1 900 mm
Width: 750 mm
Wheelbase: 1 225 mm
Clearance: 145 mm
Seat height: 750 mm
Dry weight: 89 kg
Fuel tank: 9.8 litres

Performance:
Top speed: 105 km/h
Fuel consumption: 4 l/100 km

Features: GP100U is a basic
version with wire wheels and
drum brakes.

SUZUKI (Japan)

Model: CS80 Roadie

Engine: 2-str reed valve single
Capacity: 79 cc
Bore × Stroke: 49 × 42 mm
Compression ratio: 7.2:1
Carburettor: 14 mm Mikuni
Maximum power: 5 bhp
(DIN) at 5 500 rpm
Starting: electric/kick

Transmission: 3-speed with
automatic clutch

Electrics: Transistorised 12 v
ignition with 5 Ah battery

Frame: Monocoque

Suspension: Trailing link with
rear oil dampened swinging
arm

Manufacturer: Suzuki Motor Co. Ltd.

Brakes: Drums front and rear

Tyres: 3.50–10
front and rear

Dimensions:
Length: 1 705 mm
Width: 650 mm
Wheelbase: 1 155 mm
Clearance: 100 mm
Seat height: ...
Dry weight: 73 kg
Fuel tank: 4 litres

Performance:
Top speed: 72 km/h
Fuel consumption: 2.6 l/100 km

Features: Series includes
CS50 and CS125 scooters.

SUZUKI (Japan)

Model: FR80

Engine: 2-str reed valve single
Capacity: 79 cc
Bore × Stroke: 49 × 42 mm
Compression ratio: 6.7:1
Carburettor: 16 mm Mikuni
Maximum power: 6.8 bhp
(DIN) at 6 000 rpm
Starting: kick

Transmission: 3-speed with
automatic clutch

Electrics: 6 v flywheel
magneto ignition with 4 Ah
battery

Frame: Step-thru

Suspension: Bottom link fork,
oil dampened and rear
swinging arm

Brakes: Drums front
and rear

Tyres: 2.25–17 4PR
front and rear

Dimensions:
Length: 1 805 mm
Width: 665 mm
Wheelbase: 1 185 mm
Clearance: 130 mm
Seat height: ...
Dry weight: 73 kg
Fuel tank: 4 litres

Performance:
Top speed: 83 km/h
Fuel consumption: 2.6 l/100 km

Features: FR50 is smaller
engined version.

Manufacturer: Suzuki Motor Co. Ltd.

SUZUKI (Japan)

Model: ZR50S

Engine: 2-str piston port single
Capacity: 49 cc
Bore × Stroke: 41 × 37.8 mm
Compression ratio: 6.8:1
Carburettor: 16 mm Mikuni
Maximum power: 2.9 bhp (DIN) at 8 000 rpm
Starting: kick

Transmission: 5-speed with chain drive

Electrics: 6 v flywheel magneto ignition with 4 Ah battery

Frame: Tubular single cradle

Suspension: Telescopic front fork with rear oil dampened swinging arm

Manufacturer: Suzuki Motor Co. Ltd.

Brakes: Front disc and rear drum

Tyres: Front is 2.50–18
Rear is 2.75–18

Dimensions:
Length: 2 000 mm
Width: 745 mm
Wheelbase: 1 240 mm
Clearance: 170 mm
Seat height: 750 mm
Dry weight: 82 kg
Fuel tank: 7.5 litres

Performance:
Top speed: 48 km/h
Fuel consumption: 2 l/100 km

Features: ...

SUZUKI (Japan)

Model: CL50 Suzi

Engine: 2-str reed valve single
Capacity: 49 cc
Bore × Stroke: 41 × 37.4 mm
Compression ratio: 7.2:1
Carburettor: 14 mm Mikuni
Maximum power: 2.5 bhp
(DIN) at 5 000 rpm
Starting: electric option

Transmission: 2-speed with automatic clutch

Electrics: Transistorised 6 v ignition with 4 Ah battery

Frame: Monocoque

Suspension: Telescopic front fork with rear oil-dampened swing arm

Brakes: Drums front and rear

Tyres: 2.75–10 2PR front and rear

Dimensions:
Length: 1 560 mm
Width: 645 mm
Wheelbase: 1 120 mm
Clearance: 90 mm
Seat height: ...
Dry weight: 57 kg
Fuel tank: 3 litres

Performance:
Top speed: 48 km/h
Fuel consumption: 2 l/100 km

Features: Safety start system activated by front brake lever.

Manufacturer: Suzuki Motor Co. Ltd.

TOMOS (Yugoslavia)

Model: Silver Bullet A3SP

Engine: 2-str horizontal single
Capacity: 49 cc
Bore × Stroke: 38 × 49 mm
Compression ratio: 8.5:1
Carburettor: 12 mm Encarwi
Maximum power: 1,8 bhp
(DIN) at 5 500 rpm
Starting: pedal

Transmission: 2-speed with
automatic clutch

Electrics: 6 v flywheel
magneto ignition with 1.5 Ah
Ni Cd battery

Frame: Step-thru

Suspension: Telescopic front
fork with twin rear heavy duty
shocks

Brakes: 90 mm drums
front and rear

Tyres: 2.25–20
front and rear

Dimensions:
Length: 1 640 mm
Width: 665 mm
Wheelbase: 1 080 mm
Clearance: ...
Seat height: ...
Dry weight: 44 kg
Fuel tank: 4 litres

Performance:
Top speed: 48 km/h
Fuel consumption: 2 l/100 km

Features: Tomos range
includes A3ML, A3MS mopeds
and 15SLC and 14M
lightweights.

Manufacturer: Tovarna Motornih Vozil, Tomos–Smarska c. 4,
66001 Koper, p.p. 124, Yugoslavia.

TOMOS (Yugoslavia)

Tomos BT50—80 km/h 2-stroke single sports moped

Tomos ATX50—48 km/h 2-stroke single trail moped

Tomos APN6—48 km/h 2-stroke single moped with plastic tank and guards

TRIUMPH (UK)

Model: Bonneville UK

Engine: 4-str ohv parallel twin
Capacity: 744 cc
Bore × Stroke: 76 × 82 mm
Compression ratio: 7.9:1
Carburettor: 2/30 mm Amal 1.5
Maximum power: 50 bhp
(DIN) at 7 200 rpm
Starting: kick

Transmission: 5-speed with
chain drive

Electrics: Transistorised 12 v
ignition with 8 Ah battery

Frame: Duplex tubular cradle

Suspension: Telehydraulic
front fork with twin rear
hydraulic shocks

Brakes: 260 mm triple disc
system

Tyres: Front is 100/90H–19
Rear is 110/90H–18

Dimensions:
Length: 2 220 mm
Width: 686 mm
Wheelbase: 1 422 mm
Clearance: 180 mm
Seat height: 787 mm
Dry weight: 186 kg
Fuel tank: 18.2 litres

Performance:
Top speed: 180 km/h
Fuel consumption: 5.6 l/100 km

Features: USA version has
12.8 litre fuel tank.

Manufacturer: Under licence by: L. F. Harris (Rushden) Ltd.,
Units 1 & 2 Silverhills Road, Newton Abbot, Devon, England.

YAMAHA (Japan)

Model: XVZ12TD Venture

Engine: 4-str LC dohc 70°
16-valve vee-four
Capacity: 1 198 cc
Bore × Stroke: 76 × 66 mm
Compression ratio: 10.5:1
Carburettor: 4/34 mm Mikuni
Maximum power: 97 bhp
(DIN) at 7 000 rpm
Starting: electric

Transmission: 5-speed with
shaft drive

Electrics: Transistorised 12 v
ignition with 20 Ah battery

Frame: Duplex tubular cradle

Suspension: Air-assisted front
fork with rear 4-way adjustable
Monocross system

Brakes: Triple disc system
with linked braking

Tyres: Front is 120/90H–18
Rear is 140/90H–16

Dimensions:
Length: 2 470 mm
Width: 920 mm
Wheelbase: 1 610 mm
Clearance: 145 mm
Seat height: 785 mm
Dry weight: 321 kg
Fuel tank: 20 litres

Performance:
Top speed: 193 km/h
Fuel consumption: 7 l/100 km

Features: Computer controlled
levelling. Fairing contains stereo
radio and cassette

Manufacturer: Yamaha Motor Co. Ltd., Shizuoka-ken, PO Box 1,
Iwata, Japan.

YAMAHA (Japan)

Model: FJ1100

Engine: 4-str dohc 16-valve
in-line four
Capacity: 1 097 cc
Bore × Stroke: 74 × 63.8 mm
Compression ratio: 9.5:1
Carburettor: 4/36 mm Mikuni
Maximum power: 125 bhp
(DIN) at 9 000 rpm
Starting: electric

Transmission: 5-speed with
chain drive

Electrics: Transistorised 12 v
ignition with 14 Ah battery

Frame: Box section cradle

Suspension: Telescopic fork
with adjustable damping and
anti-dive and rear *Monocross*
system

Brakes: Triple disc system
with opposed-piston calipers

Tyres: Front is 120/80V–16
Rear is 150/80V–16

Dimensions:
Length: 2 230 mm
Width: 730 mm
Wheelbase: 1 490 mm
Clearance: 140 mm
Seat height: 780 mm
Dry weight: 227 kg
Fuel tank: 24.5 litres

Performance:
Top speed: 235 km/h
Fuel consumption: 7.5 l/100 km

Features: Lateral frame
concept.

Manufacturer: Yamaha Motor Co. Ltd.

YAMAHA (Japan)

Model: XJ900F

Engine: 4-str dohc YICS
in-line four
Capacity: 891 cc
Bore × Stroke: 68.5 × 60.5 mm
Compression ratio: 9.6:1
Carburettor: 4/36 mm Mikuni
Maximum power: 98 bhp
(DIN) at 9 000 rpm
Starting: electric

Transmission: 5-speed with
shaft drive

Electrics: Transistorised 12 v
ignition with 14 Ah battery

Frame: Duplex tubular cradle

Suspension: Air-assisted fork
with twin rear adjustable
shocks

Brakes: 254 mm triple disc
system with opposed piston
calipers

Tyres: Front is 100/90V–18
Rear is 120/90V–18

Dimensions:
Length: 2 215 mm
Width: 735 mm
Wheelbase: 1 480 mm
Clearance: 145 mm
Seat height: 780 mm
Dry weight: 218 kg
Fuel tank: 22 litres

Performance:
Top speed: 210 km/h
Fuel consumption: 6.5 l/100 km

Features: Yamaha Induction
Control System. Oil cooler.
Ventilated disc brakes.

Manufacturer: Yamaha Motor Co. Ltd.

YAMAHA (Japan)

Model: FZ750

Engine: 4-str LC dohc
20-valve four
Capacity: 749 cc
Bore × Stroke: 68 × 51.6 mm
Compression ratio: 11.2:1
Carburettor: 4/34 mm Mikuni
Maximum power: 102 bhp
(DIN) at 8000 rpm
Starting: electric

Transmission: 6-speed with
chain drive

Electrics: Transistorised 12 v
ignition with 14 Ah battery

Frame: Box section cradle

Suspension: Self-adjusting
front fork with rear remote
control *Monocross* system

Brakes: Triple disc system
with opposed-piston calipers

Tyres: Front is 120/80V–16
Rear is 130/80V–18

Dimensions:
Length: 2295 mm
Width: 755 mm
Wheelbase: 1485 mm
Clearance: 160 mm
Seat height: 790 mm
Dry weight: 209 kg
Fuel tank: 22 litres

Performance:
Top speed: 240 km/h
Fuel consumption: ...

Features: World's first
20-valve production engine.
Sealed cooling system. Racing
style instrumentation.

Manufacturer: Yamaha Motor Co. Ltd.

YAMAHA (Japan)

Model: XJ650 Turbo

Engine: 4-str dohc turbo
in-line four
Capacity: 653 cc
Bore × Stroke: 63 × 52.4 mm
Compression ratio: 8.2:1
Carburettor: 4/30 Mikuni
Maximum power: 90 bhp
(DIN) at 9 000 rpm
Starting: electric

Transmission: 5-speed with
chain drive

Electrics: Transistorised 12 v
ignition with 12 Ah battery

Frame: Duplex tubular cradle

Suspension: Telescopic front
fork with twin rear adjustable
hydraulic shocks

Brakes: 270 mm twin front
discs and 230 mm rear drum

Tyres: Front is 3.25V–19
Rear is 120/90V–18

Dimensions:
Length: 2 200 mm
Width: 724 mm
Wheelbase: 1 440 mm
Clearance: 134 mm
Seat height: 775 mm
Dry weight: 230 kg
Fuel tank: 19 litres

Performance:
Top speed: 210 km/h
Fuel consumption: 6.5 l/100 km

Features: Yamaha Induction
Control System. LCD function
instrumentation.

Manufacturer: Yamaha Motor Co. Ltd.

YAMAHA (Japan)

Model: XJ600

Engine: 4-str dohc YICS
in-line four
Capacity: 598 cc
Bore × Stroke: 58.5 × 55.7 mm
Compression ratio: 10:1
Carburettor: 4/32 mm Mikuni
Maximum power: 72 bhp
(DIN) at 10 000 rpm
Starting: electric

Transmission: 6-speed with
chain drive

Electrics: Transistorised 12 v
ignition with 12 Ah battery

Frame: Duplex tubular cradle

Suspension: Telescopic front
fork with rear 5-way adjustable
Monocross system

Brakes: 267 mm triple disc
system with opposed-piston
calipers

Tyres: Front is 90/90H–18
Rear is 110/90H–18

Dimensions:
Length: 2 145 mm
Width: 750 mm
Wheelbase: 1 430 mm
Clearance: 140 mm
Seat height: 790 mm
Dry weight: 188 kg
Fuel tank: 19 litres

Performance:
Top speed: 200 km/h
Fuel consumption: 6.2 l/100 km

Features: Yamaha Induction
Control System engine
management.

Manufacturer: Yamaha Motor Co. Ltd.

YAMAHA (Japan)

Model: XT600Z Ténéré

Engine: 4-str sohc 4-valve single
Capacity: 595 cc
Bore × Stroke: 95 × 84 mm
Compression ratio: 8.5:1
Carburettor: 27 mm Mikuni
Maximum power: 44 bhp (DIN) at 6 500 rpm
Starting: kick

Transmission: 5-speed with chain drive

Electrics: 12 v CDI ignition with 5 Ah battery

Frame: Tubular single cradle

Suspension: Air-assisted leading axle fork with rear *Monocross* system

Brakes: Shrouded front disc and rear drum

Tyres: Front is 3.00S–21
Rear is 4.60S–18

Dimensions:
Length: 2 195 mm
Width: 870 mm
Wheelbase: 1 440 mm
Clearance: 260 mm
Seat height: 885 mm
Dry weight: 141 kg
Fuel tank: 30 litres

Performance:
Top speed: 160 km/h
Fuel consumption: 6 l/100 km

Features: Twin choke dual carburettor. Dry sump lubrication. Paris–Dakar rally styling.

Manufacturer: Yamaha Motor Co. Ltd.

YAMAHA (Japan)

Model: RD500LC

Engine: 2-str LC reed valve YPVS vee-four
Capacity: 499 cc
Bore × Stroke: 56.4 × 50 mm
Compression ratio: 6.6:1
Carburettor: 4/26 mm Mikuni
Maximum power: 87 bhp (DIN) at 9 500 rpm
Starting: kick

Transmission: 6-speed with chain drive

Electrics: 12 v CDI ignition with 5 Ah battery

Frame: Box section cradle

Suspension: Telescopic front fork with anti-dive and rear adjustable *Monocross* system

Brakes: Triple ventilated discs with opposed piston calipers

Tyres: Front is 120/80V–16
Rear is 130/80V–18

Dimensions:
Length: 2 085 mm
Width: 705 mm
Wheelbase: 1 375 mm
Clearance: 145 mm
Seat height: 780 mm
Dry weight: 180 kg
Fuel tank: 22 litres

Performance:
Top speed: 220 km/h
Fuel consumption: 7.5 l/100 km

Features: Grand Prix replica sports. Yamaha Power Valve System to widen torque spread.

Manufacturer: Yamaha Motor Co. Ltd.

YAMAHA (Japan)

Model: XS400

Engine: 4-str dohc in-line
twin
Capacity: 399 cc
Bore × Stroke: 69 × 53.4 mm
Compression ratio: 9.7:1
Carburettor: 2/34 mm Mikuni
Maximum power: 45 bhp
(DIN) at 9 500 rpm
Starting: electric

Transmission: 6-speed with
chain drive

Electrics: Transistorised 12 v
ignition with 12 Ah battery

Frame: Tubular spine

Suspension: Telescopic front
fork with rear adjustable
Monocross system

Brakes: 267 mm front disc
and 160 mm rear drum

Tyres: Front is 3.00S–18
Rear is 4.10S–18

Dimensions:
Length: 2 040 mm
Width: 730 mm
Wheelbase: 1 375 mm
Clearance: 150 mm
Seat height: 785 mm
Dry weight: 166 kg
Fuel tank: 20 litres

Performance:
Top speed: 160 km/h
Fuel consumption: 6 l/100 km

Features: Yamaha Induction
Control System. Engine is a
stressed member in the frame.

Manufacturer: Yamaha Motor Co. Ltd.

YAMAHA (Japan)

Model: RD350F YPVS

Engine: 2-str LC reed valve
YPVS twin
Capacity: 347 cc
Bore × Stroke: 64 × 54 mm
Compression ratio: 6:1
Carburettor: 2/26 mm Mikuni
Maximum power: 59 bhp
(DIN) at 9 000 rpm
Starting: kick

Transmission: 6-speed with
chain drive

Electrics: 12 v CDI ignition
with 5 Ah battery

Frame: Duplex tubular cradle

Suspension: Air-assisted front
fork with rear 5-way adjustable
Monocross system

Brakes: 267 mm triple disc
system with opposed piston
calipers

Tyres: Front is 90/90H–18
Rear is 110/80H–18

Dimensions:
Length: 2 095 mm
Width: 690 mm
Wheelbase: 1 385 mm
Clearance: 165 mm
Seat height: 800 mm
Dry weight: 148 kg
Fuel tank: 20 litres

Performance:
Top speed: 190 km/h
Fuel consumption: 7 l/100 km

Features: Yamaha Power
Valve System fitted. Available
with or without frame-mounted
fairing.

Manufacturer: Yamaha Motor Co. Ltd.

YAMAHA (Japan)

Model: XT350

Engine: 4-str dohc 4-valve
single
Capacity: 346 cc
Bore × Stroke: 86 × 59.6 mm
Compression ratio: 9:1
Carburettor: 26 mm YDIS
Maximum power: 31 bhp
(DIN) at 7 500 rpm
Starting: kick

Transmission: 6-speed with
chain drive

Electrics: 12 v CDI ignition
with 3 Ah battery

Frame: Tubular semi-cradle

Suspension: Air-assisted front
fork with rear adjustable
Monocross system

Brakes: 245 mm front disc
and rear drum

Tyres: Front is 3.00–21
Rear is 110/80–18

Dimensions:
Length: 2 225 mm
Width: 865 mm
Wheelbase: 1 420 mm
Clearance: 275 mm
Seat height: 855 mm
Dry weight: 120 kg
Fuel tank: 12 litres

Performance:
Top speed: 150 km/h
Fuel consumption: 5.2 l/100 km

Features: Yamaha Duo Intake
System is a twin carburettor
design to give economy and
power.

Manufacturer: Yamaha Motor Co. Ltd.

YAMAHA (Japan)

Model: RD125LC II

Engine: 2-str LC reed valve
YEIS single
Capacity: 123 cc
Bore × Stroke: 56 × 50 mm
Compression ratio: 6.4:1
Carburettor: 24 mm Mikuni
Maximum power: 12.2 bhp
(DIN) at 7 500 rpm
Starting: kick

Transmission: 6-speed with
chain drive

Electrics: 12 v CDI ignition
with 5 Ah battery

Frame: Tubular single cradle

Suspension: Telescopic front
fork with rear adjustable
Monocross system

Brakes: 245 mm front disc
and 130 mm rear drum

Tyres: Front is 80/100–16
Rear is 90/90–18

Dimensions:
Length: 1 940 mm
Width: 695 mm
Wheelbase: 1 275 mm
Clearance: 165 mm
Seat height: 755 mm
Dry weight: 98 kg
Fuel tank: 13 litres

Performance:
Top speed: 120 km/h
Fuel consumption: 5 l/100 km

Features: Yamaha Energy
Induction System. Race styling.

Manufacturer: Yamaha Motor Co. Ltd.

YAMAHA (Japan)

Model: DT125LC

Engine: 2-str LC reed valve
YEIS single
Capacity: 123 cc
Bore × Stroke: 56 × 50 mm
Compression ratio: 6.8:1
Carburettor: 26 mm Mikuni
Maximum power: 12.2 bhp
(DIN) at 6 500 rpm
Starting: kick

Transmission: 6-speed with
chain drive

Electrics: 12 v CDI ignition
with 3 Ah battery

Frame: Tubular single cradle

Suspension: Leading axle
front fork with rear adjustable
Monocross system

Brakes: Front disc and rear
drum

Tyres: Front is 2.75–21
Rear is 4.10–18

Dimensions:
Length: 2 140 mm
Width: 820 mm
Wheelbase: 1 360 mm
Clearance: 285 mm
Seat height: 845 mm
Dry weight: 99 kg
Fuel tank: 10 litres

Performance:
Top speed: 115 km/h
Fuel consumption: 5 l/100 km

Features: Yamaha Energy
Induction System for a
smoother powerband. Design
based on YZ motocross racers.

Manufacturer: Yamaha Motor Co. Ltd.

YAMAHA (Japan)

Model: BL125 Beluga

Engine: 2-str reed valve single
Capacity: 123 cc
Bore × Stroke: 56 × 50 mm
Compression ratio: 7:1
Carburettor: 22 mm Mikuni
Maximum power: 12 bhp
(DIN) at 7,000 rpm
Starting: electric

Transmission: V-belt
automatic

Electrics: 12 v CDI ignition

Frame: Tubular spine

Suspension: Bottom link front
fork with twin rear hydraulic
shocks

Brakes: Labyrinth-seal
130 mm drums front and rear

Tyres: 3.50–10
front and rear

Dimensions:
Length: 1 880 mm
Width: 650 mm
Wheelbase: 1 250 mm
Clearance: 120 mm
Seat height: 770 mm
Dry weight: 92 kg
Fuel tank: 7 litres

Performance:
Top speed: 110 km/h
Fuel consumption: ...

Features: Safety start system.

Manufacturer: Yamaha Motor Co. Ltd.

YAMAHA (Japan)

Model: RXS100

Engine: 2-str reed valve YEIS
single
Capacity: 98 cc
Bore × Stroke: 50 × 50 mm
Compression ratio: 6.7:1
Carburettor: 22 mm Mikuni
Maximum power: 12 bhp
(DIN) at 8 500 rpm
Starting: kick

Transmission: 5-speed with
chain drive

Electrics: 12 v CDI ignition

Frame: Duplex tubular cradle

Suspension: Telescopic front
fork with twin rear 5-way
adjustable shocks

Brakes: Labyrinth-seal 110 mm
drums front and rear

Tyres: Front is 2.75–18
Rear is 3.00–18

Dimensions:
Length: 1 910 mm
Width: 730 mm
Wheelbase: 1 240 mm
Clearance: 150 mm
Seat height: 780 mm
Dry weight: 94 kg
Fuel tank: 9 litres

Performance:
Top speed: 115 km/h
Fuel consumption: 4.4 l/100 km

Features: Yamaha Energy
Induction System. Rocker-pedal
gear change.

Manufacturer: Yamaha Motor Co. Ltd.

YAMAHA (Japan)

Model: YB100

Engine: 2-str rotary valve
single
Capacity: 97 cc
Bore × Stroke: 52 × 45.6 mm
Compression ratio: 6.5:1
Carburettor: 20 mm Mikuni
Maximum power: 9.8 bhp
(DIN) at 5 500 rpm
Starting: kick

Transmission: 4-speed with
chain drive

Electrics: 6 v flywheel
magneto ignition with battery

Frame: Pressed steel spine

Suspension: Telescopic front
fork with twin rear hydraulic
shocks

Manufacturer: Yamaha Motor Co. Ltd.

Brakes: Labyrinth-seal
110 mm drums front and rear

Tyres: 2.50–18 4PR
front and rear

Dimensions:
Length: 1 850 mm
Width: 735 mm
Wheelbase: 1 180 mm
Clearance: 140 mm
Seat height: 785 mm
Dry weight: 84 kg
Fuel tank: 8.6 litres

Performance:
Top speed: 110 km/h
Fuel consumption: 3 l/100 km

Features: Rocker-pedal gear
change and chain guard.

YAMAHA (Japan)

Model: V80D

Engine: 2-str reed valve YEIS single
Capacity: 79 cc
Bore × Stroke: 47 × 45.6 mm
Compression ratio: 7:1
Carburettor: 15 mm Mikuni
Maximum power: 6.76 bhp (DIN) at 6 000 rpm
Starting: kick

Transmission: 3-speed with automatic centrifugal clutch

Electrics: 6 v CDI ignition

Frame: Step-thru

Suspension: Leading link front fork with twin rear dampers

Brakes: Drums front and rear

Tyres: 2.50–17 4 PR front and rear

Dimensions:
Length: 1 850 mm
Width: 660 mm
Wheelbase: 1 170 mm
Clearance: 135 mm
Seat height: 765 mm
Dry weight: 81 kg
Fuel tank: 5.3 litres

Performance:
Top speed: 75 km/h
Fuel consumption: 2 l/100 km

Features: Yamaha Energy Induction System. Series includes V50M version with smaller engine.

Manufacturer: Yamaha Motor Co. Ltd.

YAMAHA (Japan)

Model: DT50MX

Engine: 2-str reed valve single
Capacity: 49 cc
Bore × Stroke: 40 × 39.7 mm
Compression ratio: 6.6:1
Carburettor: 14 mm Mikuni
Maximum power: 3 bhp (DIN)
at 5 500 rpm
Starting: kick

Transmission: 5-speed with
chain drive.

Electrics: Flywheel magneto
6 v ignition

Frame: Tubular cradle

Suspension: Leading axle
front fork with rear *Monocross*
system

Brakes: Drums front and rear

Tyres: Front is 2.50–21
Rear is 3.00–18

Dimensions:
Length: 2 055 mm
Width: 835 mm
Wheelbase: 1 280 mm
Clearance: 260 mm
Seat height: 820 mm
Dry weight: 81 kg
Fuel tank: 8.5 litres

Performance:
Top speed: 56 km/h
Fuel consumption: 3 l/100 km

Features: Trial bike also
available with 79 cc engine
developing 6.5 bhp.

Manufacturer: Yamaha Motor Co. Ltd.

YAMAHA (Japan)

Model: RD50MX

Engine: 2-str reed valve single
Capacity: 49 cc
Bore × Stroke: 40 × 39.7 mm
Compression ratio: 6.6:1
Carburettor: 14 mm Mikuni
Maximum power: 2.9 bhp
(DIN) at 5500 rpm
Starting: kick

Transmission: 5-speed with
chain drive

Electrics: Flywheel magneto
6 v ignition

Frame: Tubular single cradle

Suspension: Telescopic front
fork with rear *Monocross*
system

Brakes: Front disc and rear
drum

Tyres: Front is 2.50–18
Rear is 2.75–18

Dimensions:
Length: 1935 mm
Width: 745 mm
Wheelbase: 1240 mm
Clearance: 170 mm
Seat height: 790 mm
Dry weight: 83 kg
Fuel tank: 13 litres

Performance:
Top speed: 55 km/h
Fuel consumption: 3.5 l/100 km

Features: Handlebar fairing.
Also available in 80 cc versions
LC and air-cooled.

Manufacturer: Yamaha Motor Co. Ltd.

YAMAHA (Japan)

Model: MS50E

Engine: 2-str reed valve single
Capacity: 49 cc
Bore × Stroke: 40 × 39.7 mm
Compression ratio: 6.5:1
Carburettor: 12 mm Mikuni
Maximum power: 2.9 bhp
(DIN) at 6 000 rpm
Starting: electric/kick

Transmission: 2-speed
automatic with shaft drive

Electrics: 6 v CDI ignition

Frame: Pressed steel

Suspension: Telescopic front
fork with twin rear shocks

Brakes: Hand-operated drums
front and rear

Tyres: Front is 2.25–14
Rear is 3.00–12

Dimensions:
Length: 1 630 mm
Width: 680 mm
Wheelbase: 1 095 mm
Clearance: 100 mm
Seat height: 690 mm
Dry weight: 58 kg
Fuel tank: 3.2 litres

Performance:
Top speed: 48 km/h
Fuel consumption: 2 l/100 km

Features: Steering lock and
safety start switch.

Manufacturer: Yamaha Motor Co. Ltd.